all the best!

Nancy Ahlrichs

Praise for *Manager of Choice*

"A practical guide that will introduce you to fresh, contemporary strategies. A 'must share' with your colleagues as you'll collectively reap the rewards of Ahlrichs's wisdom."

— **Tom Boehner, Vice President, Human Capital, Tucker Rocky Distributing**

"Should be required reading for anyone interested in having an 'edge' in a career or business in which employees are valued."

— **Robert J. Brody, President & CEO, St. Francis Hospital and Health Centers**

"A unique and inspiring book that shows how to push cultural development and change further into the organization. A must read for any manager who wants to be someone that everybody wants to work for."

— **Darlene R. Moog, Director, Organization Development and Succession Planning, Vectren Corporation**

"A must read for leaders in all industries."

— **Tom Malasto, Executive Director, St. Francis Cardiac & Vascular Care Center**

MANAGER
OF CHOICE

MANAGER
OF CHOICE

5 COMPETENCIES
FOR CULTIVATING
TOP TALENT

Nancy S. Ahlrichs

Davies-Black Publishing
Palo Alto, California

Published by Davies-Black Publishing, a division of CPP, Inc., 3803 East Bayshore Road, Palo Alto, CA 94303; 800-624-1765.

Special discounts on bulk quantities of Davies-Black books are available to corporations, professional associations, and other organizations. For details, contact the Director of Marketing and Sales at Davies-Black Publishing, 3803 East Bayshore Road, Palo Alto, CA 94303; 650-691-9123; fax 650-623-9271.

Davies-Black and colophon are registered trademarks of CPP, Inc. Microsoft and PowerPoint are registered trademarks of Microsoft Corporation. Great Place to Work is a registered trademark of Great Place to Work Institute, Inc. PlaceWare is a registered trademark of PlaceWare, Inc. Belief System of Motivation and Performance is a trademark of Thad Green.

Visit the Davies-Black Publishing web site at www.daviesblack.com.

07 06 05 04 03   10 9 8 7 6 5 4 3 2 1
Printed in the United States of America

Library of Congress Cataloging-in-Publication Data
Ahlrichs, Nancy
>   Manager of choice : 5 competencies for cultivating top talent / Nancy S. Ahlrichs.— 1st ed.
>>   p. cm.
>   Includes bibliographical references and index.
>   ISBN 0-89106-180-0
>   1. Leadership. 2. Organizational management. I. Title.

FIRST EDITION
First printing 2003

This book is dedicated to my husband, Karl,
and to the managers of choice in my life.
Both have shown me that great bounty
and opportunities can be found every day,
no matter the situation. We make our own luck!

Contents

Preface xi

About the Author xv

Introduction xvii

Part One
The New Management Reality

1 The Business Case for Becoming a Manager of Choice 3

2 Managing with Whatever It Takes (WIT) 29

3 Organizational Culture: How We Do Things Around Here 63

4 Management Metrics That Matter 89

Part Two

Developing the Five Competencies of Managers of Choice

5   Talent Scouter 107

6   Relationship Builder 131

7   Trust Builder 159

8   Skill Builder 173

9   Brand Builder 189

Conclusion: Making MOC Status a Reality 205

Notes 213

Bibliography 223

Index 227

Preface

As I was gathering material to write this book, I thought seriously about the manager of choice imperative and how it might seem overwhelming to many managers who today find themselves battling extreme circumstances. I began thinking about real-life managers of choice I've known. I would like to share a story with you about one particularly inspiring manager with whom I worked for over seven years. This story is adapted from a column I wrote for the *Indianapolis Business Journal* in 2002.

How can each of us become a manager of choice when confronted with the grim realities facing our organization and/or industry? Your company may be on a belt-tightening binge or in an unglamorous or mature industry with an uncertain future. The answer? Play the cards you're dealt! Do it with energy, imagination, enthusiasm—and a determined smile! Do it the way my department VP Dick did for several years in a worldwide printing equipment manufacturer based in Chicago after it had been acquired by a British company in 1980—following over one hundred years of family ownership.

Suddenly, nothing was "normal." The first of many poorly executed layoffs was ripping through the organization. Competition and new technology were wreaking havoc. The printing industry was transitioning from large companies to mom-and-pop operations to even copiers and computers with printers in offices. Japanese and German competitors posed significant business threats. New product rollouts, new product training—and nearly every project—had a "zero" budget.

At what seemed like the worst of times, Dick's message every day was, "This is the *best of times* because of who we are and what we can do!" Employees called his Sales Training and Development department "Camelot." Within the company of eight thousand employees, Dick was the manager of choice for whom line and staff employees alike wanted to work. He had three secrets:

1. **Hire well or not at all.** Talent is the foundation of success. Dick and all his managers had excellent interviewing skills and viewed diversity as an asset. Dick hired a team of thirty-five- to fifty-plus-year-old seasoned managers as well as fresh college grads, mothers returning to work, high school grads, and individuals from a variety of racial, ethnic, and religious backgrounds. Half were women. Eleven were left-handed. All had a sense of humor and a positive outlook.

2. **Coach individuals individually.** Relationships build trust—and they require "face time" and communication. Dick met weekly with his direct reports, and they met weekly with theirs. He knew what motivated all of his staff members and expected them to know the same about their employees. As a result, he and his managers were able to redirect unhappy or derailing employees.

These meetings were in addition to project brainstorming or themed update meetings. Milestones ("millstones" to some) were important. Performance reviews were on time. Creativity was encouraged, and everyone knew the deadlines, quality standards, and intellectual resources for assistance. Public praise and private scolding kept everyone on target. Managers often said, "Thank you," "Good job!" and "Kudos!" Respect for—and from—all employees was expected. Fun, inexpensive rewards were given for ingenuity, great ideas, and meeting mid-project milestones.

3. **Develop every employee using every means available.** Ahead of his time, Dick created a "free-agent nation" *inside* his department. No one had a chance to get bored. In the seven years I worked in the department, I had seven jobs. With zero internal training dollars available, we were cross-trained, job-shadowed, mentored, and stretched by new experiences. We shared articles and books and attended professional organization meetings and local conferences. We brought back real content and taught each other.

Positive attitudes are contagious! At a time of zero budgets, acquisitions, layoffs, and a stagnant economy, Dick showed us that there are no unsolvable problems. He coached us to quality heights that brought us internal and external awards. He cared. He smiled! As a manager of choice, he used trust, coaching, and high expectations to energize employees to produce award-winning work. Like Dick, you, too, can be a business hero and lead your department or company out of the current wilderness. Today, more than ever, we need each of you to be a true manager of choice.

About the Author

Nancy Ahlrichs knows the secret that separates organizations with high turnover and lower profits from those with high-quality services, products, and financial performance. The secret? The most profitable organizations—employers of choice—are both customer *and* employee centered. This duality of focus is delivered by managers of choice.

Ahlrichs has more than twenty years of experience in human resources, marketing, and management. As principal of EOC Strategies, LLC, she shares her management, recruiting, retention, and diversity research in her speaking and consulting. Previously she served as Director of Organizational Evolution and as Director of Marketing and Public Relations for ONEX, Inc., an Indianapolis-based high-tech solutions consulting firm with offices in the Midwest. Ahlrichs is author of *Competing for Talent: Key Recruitment and Retention Strategies for Becoming an Employer of Choice* and a contributor to *On Staffing,* and she has written numerous articles and guest columns for newspapers, journals, and online resources.

Company presidents, CFOs, senior human resources professionals, hospital and other management teams, and even plant managers have found her approach to be strategic, tactical, and, most of all, practical. Ahlrichs has spoken to hundreds of audiences and management teams in utilities, insurance, healthcare, high tech, legal, banking, government and other fields in the past five years.

Governor Frank O'Bannon named Ahlrichs a "Distinguished Hoosier" for her service to the state of Indiana, and she was named "Kiwanian of the Year 2001–2002." A Purdue graduate with both her B.A. and M.S. degrees in anthropology, she is also certified as a Senior Professional in Human Resources (SPHR). Ahlrichs served on the board of directors for a Cleveland-based high-tech human resources software development firm and is active in a variety of community and professional organizations including the Kiwanis Club of Indianapolis, the Society for Human Resource Management (SHRM), and the Association for Psychological Type (APT). Visit her website at www.eocstrategies.com.

Introduction

Imagine a work world with motivated employees, positive relationships, and greater opportunity for your own advancement. Imagine fewer fires to put out on a daily basis. Imagine employees from throughout the organization lined up to fill your open positions—competing with qualified external candidates referred by your employees. Imagine receiving the positive regard of senior management.

For a lucky few, this is not a dream, because they are managers of choice. For others, it is still an attainable goal. The purpose of this book is to move you closer to the manager of choice reality. Managers of choice (MOCs) know that learning the secrets of talent relationship management will pay off in lower turnover, rarer staff surprises, fewer headaches, more satisfied customers, and more career options.

If change also holds with it the promise of opportunity, managers have a vast opportunity in front of them—because management in the first decade of the twenty-first century is very different from what it was in the twentieth. According to Keith Greene, SPHR, director of organizational programs for the Society for Human Resource Management (SHRM), four issues are paramount in this decade: retention of talent, attraction of talent with critical skills, improved workplace performance, and the building of workforce skills.[1] One-size-fits-all management approaches are no longer effective, he says, because "the new rule of motivation is 'everyone is different.'"

America's strength has always been its diversity, so the way the workplace has evolved should come as no big surprise. While the "Leave It to Beaver" family of working dad and mom at home with two kids has not been the model for years, Greene illustrates why traditional approaches to recruiting, performance management, training, and retention have ceased to be effective:

- **The workforce is no longer young.** Starting in 2001, there are now more employees over the age of 40 than under 40 (AARP); by 2010, the population between the ages of 35 and 44 will shrink 10.2 percent (Bureau of Labor Statistics).

- **More women are working.** Forty-eight percent of the workforce will be female by 2008 (Department of Labor).

- **Knowledge of at least some Spanish is helpful.** Hispanics will become the largest U.S. minority by 2005 (U.S. Census Bureau).

- **Religious accommodations are more common.** Christianity (Protestants and Catholics combined) is the largest religious group, but Islam is surpassing Judaism as the second-largest group.

- **Eldercare is more of an issue.** The 25 percent of the working population with eldercare responsibilities cause their organizations to lose $29 billion annually in productivity due to missed work, changed schedules, and declined promotions.

- **Alternative work schedules are not just for parents.** Twenty percent of those who seek flexible schedules are childless. Sixty-four percent of workers would rather have four ten-hour days than five eight-hour days (Hart Research).

- **Overtime and long hours are not welcome, as time is valued more than money by many employees.** Sixty-one percent of adults—including 70 percent of men surveyed—say that they would give up some of their pay for more time with their family (Radcliffe Public Policy Center). Seventy percent of employees don't think they have a healthy balance between work and personal life (True Careers Survey).

Let's get real: management was never easy! You would not be searching for new management tools, however, if you were not already a leader. This book is for managers who believe that more is possible—not just doing more with less. You want more learning, trust, quality, fun—and satisfaction at the end of the day. This book is for the manager who wants to inspire innovation and creativity and who wants to be part of the next wave of growth.

Every organization is focused on profitability and uncovering the business truths that will help it more easily achieve its strategic goals. One of those truths is that becoming an "employer of choice" has a positive financial impact—but it cannot be a stand-alone strategy. There are no employers of choice (EOCs) without managers of choice (MOCs). Managers are the implementers of EOC practices. While strategy and technology can enable employees, only MOCs open the door to top performance.

As I wrote in my book *Competing for Talent: Key Recruitment and Retention Strategies for Becoming an Employer of Choice,* the role of the manager is crucial to implementing the six foundation strategies for becoming an employer of choice:

1. **Add improved recruiting and retention to the strategic plan of the organization; set measurable objectives for each supervisor, manager, director, and vice president.** This is *not* solely a senior management responsibility. MOCs set and achieve recruiting and retention objectives. Managers strongly influence recruiting and retention successes through interview preparation, selection criteria, speed to hire, assimilation, development, etc.

2. **Build and communicate a top-employer reputation.** This is *not* the sole responsibility of the Marketing Communications department. MOCs regularly talk about organizational culture—and their staffs echo the statements inside and outside the walls. The layering effect develops and reinforces the employment brand.

3. **Hire well—or not at all.** This is *not* the sole responsibility of the Human Resources department! As a hiring manager, you must accept that the buck stops with you! Become known as a manager who only hires *top talent*—what "Corporate Curmudgeon" columnist and author Dale Dauten refers to in *The Gifted Boss* as "the Wild Brains, the original thinkers, the self-reliants."[2] For top talent, your being selective means that they have the opportunity to work with other top talent—and that is a magnet for the best candidates in any job category.

4. **Treat employees as if they were customers.** Star treatment is *not* just for external customers. Your employees have more job and career choices than your customers have service or product choices. MOCs learn to listen to their employees and to treat them all like the organization's best customers want to be treated: with respect.

5. **Retrain and develop current employees for tomorrow's needs.** This is *not* solely a Training and Development department responsibility. Even Fortune 500 companies know that continuous learning can be accomplished on a shoestring budget. MOCs never stop teaching—or learning!

6. **Build support processes to ensure ongoing success of the six foundation strategies.** This is *not* solely a senior management responsibility. "Use it or lose it" applies to muscles, cultural elements, and business processes alike. Your actions and input keep the EOC momentum going forward.

You can be the first MOC in an organization to raise the bar by setting a goal of becoming an EOC, or you can be the next MOC within an EOC organization to take it to the greater heights required by our changing business environment.

This book is divided into two parts: "The New Management Reality" and "Developing the Five Competencies of Managers of Choice." The stage is set in chapter 1, "The Business Case for Becoming a Manager of Choice." It outlines three external drivers of change that are fueling the need for innovation and strong people management skills at all levels of management within organizations. The financial benefit of managing both people and the numbers has been shown to far surpass that accrued by managing just the numbers.

In chapter 2, "Managing with Whatever It Takes (WIT)," the trends and demographic drivers behind the need for alternative work configurations are reviewed as well as the variety of work and employee configurations that will be used to get results. To help ensure success when not all employees are under one roof working together, the importance of success stories, communication, mentoring, and "managing up" is explored.

Chapter 3, "Organizational Culture: How We Do Things Around Here," brings home the concept of the manager as the culture personified. Culture is a "people magnet"—and so are managers of choice. To attract the quality and quantity of people desired, managers must learn how to communicate the culture inside and outside the organization, use culture to inspire innovation and deliver profitability, and expand their capabilities through peer mentoring.

Chapter 4, "Management Metrics That Matter," the final chapter in part 1, covers how MOCs redefine their performance management goals and metrics to align with the strategic goals of the organization. A variety of metrics are discussed to help you track the processes that together will add up to successful outcomes for you and your organization.

Part 2 is devoted to the five competencies needed to attract and manage top talent. Chapter 5, "Talent Scouter," covers the fundamental competency that sets managers and managers of choice apart. Ordinary managers hope that the right person will walk in the door, while MOCs know that they make their own luck in the area of staffing by seeking, spotting, and hiring diverse top talent for their human capital portfolio.

Chapter 6, "Relationship Builder," focuses on capturing "heartshare" as well as "mindshare" to be able to influence the discretionary effort of employees. A committed employee will outperform a merely competent one. The discussion includes relationship building with new hires before day one and the importance of relationship building among employees and with other departments, as well as how to build relationships with the external community, coach employees to maximize performance, and use technology to enhance relationships.

At a time when having a job is not a motivator for either top performance or retention—and being "grateful to have a job" is not part of the employment gestalt, the management truths discussed in chapter 7, "Trust Builder" are more important than ever. Building—or rebuilding—trust through deliberate modeling of the organization's values and continuous communication, as well as the importance of trust as the enabler for positive work–life balance programs, is covered in this chapter.

Continuous learning cannot take place just in a classroom. Chapter 8, "Skill Builder," looks at where and how MOCs are training their staffs. Continuous learning in our knowledge economy requires a variety of source media and enables the creation of an internal "free-agent nation" for employees—and for you.

Chapter 9, "Brand Builder," brings home what every manager has come to understand: the ethical actions of a few determine the success or failure of even the most well-known organizations. The discussion includes how organizational brands work with employment brands, how your organization's brands affect quality, efficiency, innovation, and creativity, and how MOCs collaborate with their HR and Marketing partners to go beyond organizational and employment brands to attract top talent.

Years of layoffs and the terrorist attacks of September 11 as well as job and career choice have ended traditional long-term loyalty. Employees today are true to themselves, their families, and their chosen fields. While Americans no longer identify as closely with their jobs or their employers, they do relate closely to their immediate managers. Due to tight supply and high demand for top talent, managers must provide a positive work experience to attract employees who will care about, give 100 percent to, and remain with an employer. You are the person in charge of your employees' day-to-day work experience. In this decade, MOCs will be the ones chosen by their employees—and rewarded by senior management. Managers of choice will transform their employers into employers of choice.

Part One
The New Management Reality

The Business Case
for Becoming a
Manager of Choice

"Because that's where the money is."

—**Willie Sutton,** bank robber, on why he robbed banks

Today, we must manage better than anyone ever managed us. Managing better requires specific competencies, but first it requires that we defy the voice in our head that sneers, "No one ever did that for me," or, "Don't ask questions—just do it." Because the loudest voice in our head says, "You can't make money managing people," we must struggle to resist the temptation to use the "manage the numbers" approach—the silver bullet that once guaranteed productivity and profitability, back when qualified employment candidates significantly outnumbered available jobs and efficiency was top priority.[1] We have learned the hard way that "when undue attention is focused on a single figure, undue effort is devoted to manipulating it."[2] Accounting scandals, ethical lapses, and the stock market

3

repercussions have shown that managing numbers instead of people did not work before and it does not work now.

We are in the midst of three dramatic external changes that are
driving strategy in organizations of any size, in any American location, in any industry or sector:

- **Demographics.** American workplaces are rapidly beginning to
  mirror those around the globe. Workforce demographics are
  changing by every measure: gender, race, national origin, religion, age, and so on. Simultaneously, a shortage of top talent is
  emerging. According to the U.S. Bureau of Labor Statistics, our
  organizations will need to fill 55 million positions over the
  next decade, but only 29 million employees will be available!
  This 26 million shortfall will affect all employers, some much
  more than others.[3]

- **The transformation of the employee from a liability to an asset.**
  With fewer workers available, top talent is prized today more
  than ever before. Management guru Peter Drucker says, "The
  only difference between one organization and another is the
  performance of its people"; distinguished business author and
  professor Gary Hamel goes one step further: "People are *all*
  there is to an organization."[4]

  Throughout this book we uncover how demographics,
  world events, and generational differences are transforming
  employees at all levels into "consumers of the work experience." In-demand, highly skilled employees want a tailored
  work experience, often with an atypical work configuration.
  Teamed with Human Resources' access to "best practices," the
  midlevel and frontline manager are crucial to making available
  customized rewards, intangible as well as tangible, keyed to
  specific work groups and individuals.

- **The rising importance of an organization's employment brand.**
  The positive public perception of a product or service, that is, its

brand (or reputation for the experience that the consumers can expect)—which attracts customers and drives financial performance—will increasingly depend on the organization's *employment* brand (or reputation for the experience *employees* can expect). When the lack of senior management ethics can shatter a nation's economy more than terrorist acts, the importance of an organization's reputation for quality products and services, as well as ethical business practices, is clear. How employees are treated helps determine how they treat customers, make products, and deliver services. Making branding statements a reality is a key component of ongoing financial success and it is a part of the manager's role. Later we discuss who is doing it well—and how.

Those three external changes are driving the need for two equally dramatic organizational strategic changes:

- **Senior management's new mandate is for innovation and new product or service creation.** While process-focused quality initiatives and efficiency efforts dominated the end of the nineties, today quick innovation to meet changing customer needs is critical for organizational growth and stability. While the cultures that encourage listening and creativity are in many ways in opposition to those that focus on quality and efficiency, listening and creativity are requirements for satisfying customers and staying competitive in a global, high-tech world. Managing for innovation is an exciting new quest.

- **People management is the new core competency.** Today, people management is a must at every level of management. Managers who previously focused on processes, project management, and budgets will need to add considerable people management skills to their repertoire in order to engage their staffs and release their creativity. Later in this chapter (and in more depth in part 2), we discuss the new management competencies that make up the people management–profit link.

Demographics Determine Staffing Strategy

Who will be managed in the twenty-first century? The statistics are surprising. Barring unforeseeable wars, outbreaks of incurable diseases, or unexpected increases in immigration, America's workforce will increase by only 1 percent per year until 2005, according to Richard W. Judy and Carol D'Amico in *Workforce 2020*—then the rate of increase will fall to .03 percent until 2010.[5] Through 2020, workforce growth, according to the U.S. Labor Department, is expected to shrink. The number of jobs available already dwarfs the number of qualified employees in nearly every field from healthcare to teaching to engineering. High-quality talent will become increasingly scarce and increasingly diverse inside our borders while a global surplus of skills grows outside our borders.

Demographic changes are driving changes in management approaches. Now that employers line up for job candidates, employees can easily change their tasks and even entire careers, not to mention income levels. With so many more jobs available than qualified candidates, managers can no longer motivate performance by speaking softly (or loudly or not at all) or by carrying a big stick. Motivating employees to ever-higher levels of productivity by using "war jargon," pounding on desks, or invoking the names of current or past football coaches no longer works. Colorful posters with thoughtful quotes get no response. Even saying "just do it" does not get it done well. The effectiveness of old-style command-and-control managers is shrinking as quickly as the market for Elvis, Beatles, and Frank Sinatra memorabilia,[6] thanks to

- The retirement of so-called Veteran generation employees and the early retirement of Baby Boomers in management and non-management functions (up to 60 percent plan to retire early)[7]

- The accelerated acceptance of family as a top priority among employees of both genders and all generations following the shocking attacks of September 11

- The scarcity of Generation X and Generation Y hires who are interested in working in a typical twentieth-century work environment

- The need for more of the future workforce to come from outside the "developed" countries[8]—today, the employment market-place in the U.S. consists of more immigrants than at any time since the 1920s

The current lack of people management skills puts most managers and entire organizations at a severe disadvantage, especially in marketplaces with considerable competition for top talent and for customers. Today's multiethnic, four-generation workforce has different needs, goals, and motivators—and the best employees among them have multiple opportunities to be successful as employees elsewhere, or even as entrepreneurs.

As managers with products to manufacture, services to deliver, medical miracles to perform, buildings to build, cases to win, and so on, our challenge is to attract, hire, engage, develop, and retain the best talent from each generation, no matter what their other differences. This requires looking at the management job differently and looking at our staffs differently.

The Evolution of Employees from "Liabilities" to "Assets"

Employees have been seen as liabilities ever since Henry Ford lamented, "Every time I hire two hands, a head comes with them." Employees with ideas back then were not seen as assets, that is, the source of future improvements, products, growth, or profits. Though revolutionary for his time, the founding Ford was also the ultimate controlling manager who wanted employees to do exactly as they were told, no more and no less. He did not want employees to engage their minds, anticipate problems, or offer ideas. Ford's archaic approach lives on in today's managers who mistakenly believe that "you just can't find good people any more" who will "just do it" without asking questions.[9]

While publicly exclaiming, "Employees are our greatest asset," number-focused senior managers do not "walk the talk" of an employees-as-assets culture by providing the procedures, metrics, or rewards to support that statement. While metrics may be used to track the value of a specific customer's business, they are rarely used to track the savings and profit contributions of high-performing, long-term employees—or excellent managers. With the exception of the sales staff, whose only measure that matters is sales per person, too few employees have their numerous contributions tracked. To find and keep good people requires that you value employees differently and track their contributions using new metrics.

In reality, "A" players in any function—not just those employees in "sales generator" or billable positions—create from 80 percent to 130 percent more value than "C" players.[10] "A" players are found at any level within an organization and include

- Innovators with new product or service ideas

- Loyal employees who source high-quality new hires or refer potential customers

- "Opinion leaders" who effortlessly mentor new employees and bond together everyone in their department during tough times

- Role-model employees who consistently provide quality manufacturing of products or delivery of services

Even using so-called performance management standards, too few managers quantify productive, long-term employees as assets and a source of long-term profits. Instead of identifying and rewarding consistently strong contributors, managers—and typical processes—focus on identifying the weakest link among the staff. Because of this strong negative focus, managers often neglect to nurture the contributors among the other 90 percent of their

What's Working at the Space Coast Credit Union

Tracking turnover while also adding management rewards for better management practices or better employee performance gets positive results. The Space Coast Credit Union, a 250-employee organization, reduced annual employee turnover from 62% to 39% in one year, to 31% in two years, and to 17% in three years. Merchandise and trips rewarded the eleven managers with 100% employee retention.[11]

employees—which loosens their bonds to the organization. Like neglected customers, unappreciated employees vote with their feet—and may take others with them. If the top performers are the ones who walk away because of lack of attention and recognition for their consistent contributions, it is often difficult or impossible to replace them with equal or better talent.

Turnover makes the manager's job more difficult in many ways. In an attempt to lower turnover and to be seen as an employer of choice (EOC), many organizations track voluntary employee turnover by manager and hold managers responsible. Management bonuses may be in part determined by turnover metrics—managers may be punished for losing staff—but many managers lack the knowledge or tools to deal with the problem. Different metrics and incentives are needed to spotlight value-added employee contributions, as well as to highlight the best people managers. The "What's Working" example above demonstrates the benefits of using rewards to lower employee turnover.

As employees are finally coming to be seen as assets, managers must develop new metrics to measure each employee's value to the organization. To maximize the potential of your organization's EOC efforts, it may be up to you to develop your own relationship management skills—and to convince senior management and Human

Resources to use asset metrics combined with rewards for people management successes. As you will see later in this book, it can be done!

Employees: New Consumers of the Work Experience

Labor—whether highly credentialed or unskilled—can be best viewed in the context of a market driven by demand and supply. Due to shrinking demographics and ever-expanding global markets, demand exceeds the available supply of labor in a majority of fields. Poor people management approaches actually repel top talent. This is a radical concept to large corporations, prestigious law firms, well-known hospitals, big accounting firms, family-owned dynasties, and other heretofore highly respected employers that have counted on their previously magnetic brands of quality products or services to attract both customers and employees. Product and service brands alone are no longer effective in attracting top talent. Shocked by the September 11 terrorist attacks and subsequent corporate scandals, on top of the downsizings in the 1980s and 1990s, many young entrepreneurial employees have almost no interest in working for large corporations, big law firms, or even high-profile local employers because of bureaucracy and "one-size-fits-all" management approaches. Even Baby Boomers have shifted their characteristic "work first, family second" priorities. Retaining "A" players of any age—and attracting more employees like them—will require strategies that intellectually or emotionally engage workers at all levels. Refusal to be flexible will repel the top talent needed to provide high-quality products and services and profitability.

Thanks to the convergence of demographics, job and career choice, new family focus, business scandals, and an expanding economy, we have a true buyer's job market, with employees as job buyers and employers as job sellers. Employees and job candidates respond to behavioral triggers such as an organization's employment brand and employment value proposition. Word on the chat room street tells them what it is like to work for almost any organization. The behavioral rules for attracting or repelling consumers now apply to employees—now the consumers of the work experience.

The manager–employee relationship has been similar to that between the company and customer, with the company on top and the employee and the customer on the bottom. Historically, companies developed products or services to their own specifications, defined the features, decided how to market them, and decided when to make changes or to remove products from the marketplace. Companies "implicitly linked cost reduction and internal efficiencies to value creation."[12] In other words, the company defined what the customer should and would value about the product or service. It worked for years because customers had fewer choices.

Until recently, managers likewise defined everything about the work experience of employees, from job content and salary to the work environment and length of service. Table 1 illustrates the traditional approach used by companies to define and communicate the value of the product or service to the buyer, and the approach of managers to define and communicate the value of the job to the employee. As twenty-first-century consumers, however, both customers and employees now demand a different model, one that gives them a voice in defining the meaning of value.

Customers now judge products or services in terms of their experiences throughout the process of inquiry, purchase, use, follow-up service, and decision to repurchase. Just as competitive pricing of products or services ceased to be enough once there were more choices for potential buyers, competitive wages and benefits are no longer enough for current and potential employees who have abundant job and career choices—including the choice to be a free agent. The increasingly competitive market demands an employment and management strategy that enables the attraction,

Table 1 Traditional Value Definitions	
Ways Companies Define Products	**Ways Managers Define Jobs**
Features and Descriptions	**Responsibilities and Descriptions**
Advertised availability (current clients only, limited-time offers, with coupon, television infomercials, Internet pop-up boxes, multiple print and electronic media, etc.)	Advertised availability (in-house intranet listings, word of mouth only, external posting only, multiple internal and external media postings, etc.)
Price (including variety of prices depending on the distributor or product/service configuration, etc.)	Salary/wages (including variety of wage ranges depending on tenure, skill sets, etc.)
Frills (extra features available to specific buyers, sometimes "free" and sometimes for additional cost)	Benefits (health insurance, paid vacation days, paid time off or personal days, uniforms, free parking, childcare vouchers, etc.)
Purchase availability (24/7, Monday–Friday, 8:00 a.m.–5 p.m., "not sold in stores," etc.)	Work hours/availability of work (full-time, part-time, 40 hours, regular overtime, etc.)
Sale environment (Internet, catalogue only, retail outlets, with or without sales rep contact, etc.)	Work environment/culture (one site, multiple sites, telecommuting, regular meetings with manager, etc.)
Additions or changes (model changes, colors, sizes, quantity, bundling or unbundling of features, timing of changes, etc.)	Content additions or changes (static or expanded responsibilities, use of technology, ongoing process improvement or elimination, timing of changes, etc.)
Length of product use (one-time use, recyclable, 100,000-mile warranty, built-in obsolescence, etc.)	Length of employment per position (fast-track position, contract, dead-end position, development position, etc.)
Product/service retirement (planned phaseout, pulled from the marketplace for lack of profitability, geographic availability, updating or replacement with better technology, etc.)	Position retirement (job elimination, job relocation, outsourcing, "reorganized out," job sharing, etc.)

development, and mobilization of talent to sustain a competitive advantage. To be successful, managers must offer flexibility, speed of response, and individual manager–employee relationships in the complex hiring marketplace.[13]

If today's product or service buyer's definition of value is ignored, profits will be negatively affected. For example, service consumers might want all documentation related to a purchased service to be printed on their own company letterhead as if the source of the information were internal. Or, thanks to the Internet's twenty-four-hour accessibility, clothing buyers might want the option to buy at 3 a.m. or to order an item of clothing in a color unavailable at their local "bricks and mortar" store. In other words, the standard offering may be valued only if it is customized. Otherwise, customers will be out the door—and your profitability and growth plans will go out with them.

In similar ways, today's employee has become a discriminating consumer of the work experience who wants a customized work arrangement. Each employee in an organization's diverse population has a different view of what it will take to engage him or her in any work relationship. Managers complain, "If I make exceptions for one employee, I'll have to do it for all employees," but making exceptions will increasingly become the key to keeping top talent.

Different life stages may influence employee preferences for full-time, part-time, or shift work, or telecommuting, job-sharing, project-based, or other work configurations. Fewer and fewer employees find the traditional, rigid set of rules and policies attractive. Sufficient job choices exist today for employees to select for flexibility or a variety of other exceptions. Top talent is most attracted to employers of choice, those who are known for their positive treatment of employees.

The Employment Brand Determines the Product or Service Brand

Marketers know that a positive perception of a product or service brand requires that the customer have a positive experience not just with the organization's product or service, but also throughout *every* encounter with the organization's employees. This is the new reality in a world of product and service choices. Similarly, the employment brand depends on the total employee work experience. As a manager, your approach to people management determines whether you are an organization brand builder—or an organizational brand killer.

Every day as a manager, you get up in the morning and decide to be or not to be a better manager. "How?" is the question. Because managers are the key to the quality of employees' work experience, managers are the key to the employment brand. What you say, do, instruct, question, allow, punish, ignore, recognize, reward, and promote takes you, your staff, and your organization down one of three paths: to solid mediocrity, to Enron-Andersen business hell, or to EOC ingenuity, respect, and prosperity.

Attracting, managing, and retaining the best talent from all four generations is no small task. Employees from each generation demand to be managed as individuals—not as work groups, age groups, or functions. A review of the demographics of the different generations shows that *younger* also means more diverse in terms of gender, race, national origin, religion, sexual orientation, marital status, individual expression, and desire for control over work schedule, location, and configuration—and more! Your challenge is to enable a wide range of diverse employees to have a positive work experience so that they will deliver a positive product or service experience to the customer. Exceptions will become the rule. Successful people management will require managing people fairly but not alike. You can learn these skills.

Innovation Is Riveting Senior Management's Focus

Demographic changes, the new view of employees as consumers, and the role of managers as brand builders all signal the end of business as usual. To extend the growth phase of products, services, and entire organizations beyond twenty-five years in the face of global hypercompetition and increased commoditization,[14] or lack of uniqueness, senior management teams know they must go beyond quality and efficiency. Technology alone will not provide the answer. The focus for senior management in this decade is new product development and innovation.[15] According to Gary Hamel, "To thrive in turbulent times, a company must do more than retrench: it must give customers new and compelling reasons to spend; it must reinvent its cost structure; it must rebuild new growth platforms that leverage its competencies and assets. All that takes innovation."[16] Hector de J. Ruiz, CEO at Advanced Micro Devices, concurs: "[Economic] slowdown gives companies the opportunity to innovate. The engine of real economic growth is not technology but innovation. And only the companies who are customer-centric in their innovation will succeed."[17] Finally, a headline printed over Microsoft chairman Bill Gates's photo on the cover of the June 2002 issue of *Business 2.0* screams the message to managers: "How to Beat Him: Innovate!"

The innovation wrought by top talent, intellectual property, and talent relationship management allows businesses to more quickly customize or expand offerings, enter new markets, and more. The employee skills required to achieve this new business agenda will not materialize, however, without the participation of great people managers.

Management's Job Description
Now Includes "People Management"

Too often, managers are the only ones in the organization who are hired and rewarded even when they cannot fulfill the promise of their job title: manage people. Chances are, neither you nor your boss were hired or promoted for your stellar people management skills. What percentage of your peers are good people managers? Probably less than 50 percent. And "talent relationship management," as people management is often called, is truly a new frontier.

People management has, in fact, rarely been a qualification for manager selection, an expectation of manager performance, or any part of the manager reward or recognition processes in most organizations. Historically, most managers were selected from among the best performers or those who simply hung on long enough. Many of today's managers are the product of poor people managers themselves. Generations of managers have been trained using the sink-or-swim approach. Not to be confused with true management training, this approach could be used top to bottom throughout the organization because so many qualified staff replacements were lined up eagerly waiting for their opportunity. If a manager at any level did not perform well, replacements were as available as running water from a faucet. Managers could simply be told to manage in whatever way they wanted to get needed performance from staff.

Budget planning and budget management have been taught, facilitated, and rewarded, but not people management. Traditionally, little training has been provided to managers, who have instead been instructed to hire employees who "don't need managing." This has made it easier for managers to believe that "doing a good job should be its own reward," so they could just leave employees alone: no feedback, pats on the back, or recognition. In this situation, the onus weighs heavily on the employee to "make the job work out." Fear of being replaced then ensures that little employee–manager interaction is expected. Managers parroted the idea that career development is up to the employee and were surprised when so many of them job-hopped their way to knowledge. Once demographic changes and economic growth enabled widespread job choice, the lack of people management skills caused unnecessarily high levels of expensive employee turnover—thus proving that you can lose money by managing people poorly.

It is time to recognize the importance of the people manager side of manager responsibilities. The tidal wave of early retirements, immigration, and other demographic changes that will transform the employee populations of our organizations have become the impetus for many individual managers as well as senior management of the best organizations to raise their expectations about manager selection, development, and performance management processes. They realize that human capital management skills are critical to the success of the business. Being a great people manager also differentiates you from your peers—and it will add enjoyment to your job. By improving your people management skills, you will improve your productivity, your staff's productivity, and your employee retention rate. To win the competition for talent, and to succeed in a business world where new product development, innovation and flexibility—not just quality and efficiency—determine the customer's perception of value, you must hasten your own development into a new kind of management hero. The ability to understand the people—in addition to the numbers, the projects, and the customers—sets apart both managers and organizations as managers of choice and employers of choice, respectively.

The Manager of Choice Defined

A manager of choice (MOC) is the one chosen by employees who can work elsewhere and for other managers. An MOC is the one chosen by senior management to handle increasing levels of responsibility and authority. An MOC is even chosen by prospective employees inside and outside the organization who know managers through their accomplishments and through the words of those who work with them. As an MOC, you, too, can experience the benefits of 360-degree support in your work world.

Better people management starts with figuring out what needs to be done and looking at the work with new eyes—and seeing more than one way to do it. It requires you to understand your central role in the culture, or how the work is done, because as far as your employees are concerned, *you* are the organization's culture. To activate the organization's values and mission in their own job, employees must experience the values through you. Values posted on walls or included in performance management standards are not experienced and understood in terms that apply to their job level and responsibilities. Without witnessing the values modeled by you, employees cynically experience the organization's values as nothing more than words.

Additionally, being an MOC requires you to consistently excel in the following five competencies:

- **Talent scouting.** You are the gatekeeper for the quality of talent in your corner of the organization. Those who are hired are part of your organization's human capital portfolio. Clearly, nothing happens without talent—preferably top talent for whatever the work. In addition to partnering with the HR department, you must take an active role in the entire talent acquisition process. Today, talent scouting requires more than a hasty review of resumes, getting interviews on the calendar, and making a selection decision. The best talent is out there— MOCs learn how to get more than their share by becoming involved in the sourcing as well as the selection process. Prospective candidates may be drawn to a specific organization because of its product or service brand, but they bond to a specific manager and what they perceive as the employment brand. It is the manager who ignites their enthusiasm for the job, ensures that they accept the offer of employment and, once hired, stay. MOCs are integral to every element of the hiring process.

- **Relationship building**. To each of your direct reports, you are the most important person in the organization. Thirty percent of employees change jobs to get away from their managers[18]— the most important relationship for an employee is the one with his or her manager. Once you have the talent hired for the work to be done, assimilation, orientation, relationship development, and coaching are needed to bring out the best in your people and to help your work group to interact throughout your larger organization or even in the community. Relationship building with each of your reports is key to being the manager you always wanted to have and always wanted to be.

- **Trust building.** A divisive "us versus them" atmosphere is not only mentally exhausting, but it also takes up "mindshare" that could be used for new product or service development. You are the one who determines whether staff see themselves as members of a team, as team members who are part of a larger organizational entity, and as members of the larger community that includes customers, prospects, vendors, future hires, and families. With positive relationships comes trust—two-way trust. With trust, there is the opportunity for creative spark and innovation. Today's employees will not stay in an organization that does not trust them to make decisions or bring ideas to the table.

- **Skill building.** In your role as manager, you are expected to teach and to make learning available. To ensure that both management and staff are market competitive in today's "knowledge economy," constant learning is essential—otherwise, the organization is on the fast track to obsolescence. The marketplace is changing, technology is changing, your field is changing, and even your organization is changing. Neither you nor your work group can afford to be left behind.

- **Organization brand building.** You are the keeper of the truth about the brand of your organization. The employment brand (what employees experience at the organization) determines the perception of the product or service brand. Your employees cannot deliver better customer treatment than they receive as employees. Unless you continuously reinforce the values and behaviors desired of all employees, and unless you shine a bright light on those who deserve recognition for living the organization's values, your organization's branding statements (what it is like for the customer to use your services or product) will be meaningless.

Employers of Choice Exist Thanks to Managers of Choice

Employees and managers alike want to work for the top employer—the employer of choice (EOC)—in their geographic area, industry, or function. Nearly all managers and human resource professionals have heard of it; they just don't know how to achieve it. They know that there are informal lists of EOCs in their own cities—both in the media and in the minds of their employees, peers inside and outside the organization, area school counselors, university professors, and others in their industry. Industry-specific and national EOC lists also exist. *Fortune* magazine's "100 Best Companies to Work For" in America is considered to be the premier EOC list. Though originally self-nominated, the organizations on *Fortune*'s annual list have credibility as EOCs because their claims have been validated by thorough research and a random survey of 250 of their own employees.

EOC status is conferred on an organization that is "able to meet growth and profitability goals because it attracts and retains the quality and quantity of employees it needs."[19] EOCs—those employers who come to mind when we are dreaming of success for ourselves and our children—have a cadre of managers of choice (MOCs) who handle the daily execution of business strategy. An organization cannot simply declare itself an EOC—but it can declare the *goal* of becoming an EOC and initiate the processes and tactics to develop an EOC reputation! MOCs are a key ingredient that separates "wanna-bes" from the organizations on *Fortune*'s "100 Best Companies to Work For" list. EOCs cannot exist without MOCs.

Making the Leap to an Employer of Choice

Reputation combined with experience creates the brand. Your organization's product or service brand—and its employment brand—attracts or repels prospects, customers, and job candidates and can bond together or alienate current employees. Whether positive or negative, brands last a long time, so being conscious of developing a positive brand is part of building the business. A study of organizations listed as among the "100 Best Companies to Work For" from 1983 to 1997 found that corporate reputations tend to endure— whether good or bad—and cause companies to remain in either the top or bottom ten of the survey year after year.[20]

Engaged employees and managers want their organization to experience the pride and profitability of being a career destination for top talent. They realize, however, that if their current reputation is one of old-style, inflexible, one-size-fits-all management, their organization will not attract and retain the best from among today's multigenerational and increasingly diverse workforce. To gain the competitive edge that will take them through changes caused by mergers, acquisitions, and seesaw economies and provide the quality level of products and services demanded by customers with global options, employers need to develop MOCs in order to become EOCs. Top talent is attracted to EOCs. While senior-level management sets the strategy, midlevel and frontline managers are the engine that powers an organization-wide EOC strategy to reality. The best among those managers are MOCs.

Most managers want to work for an EOC but may only work for a "wanna-be." Don't let that hold you back from self-development. Your self-development efforts will fuel your organization's trajectory toward EOC status. You are empowered to develop yourself and to think and act strategically. This book assumes that you have access to industry-specific technical skills training as well as "finance for nonfinancial managers"–type training or other traditional financial management skills resources. What you need is access to skills resources focused on effective, nontraditional people management.

What is better people management in a time of insufficient qualified people, abundant job choices, and constant financial pressure along with economic uncertainty? What does it take to be seen as a top manager whose staff delivers top performance? What does it take to have people lined up at your door who want to work for *you?* Think about the manager you wanted earlier in your career—but gave up wanting. Better people management skills may even be what you wish your own manager would exhibit with you right now.

The People Management–Profit Link

There is a strong relationship between employee turnover, customer turnover, and profitability. Since you are responsible for profitability in your corner of the organization, it is important to understand the people management–profit link. Longtime, knowledgeable employees deliver a higher-quality product or service, resulting in the customer's high-quality overall experience. In contrast, even the most credentialed new employees often function at well below capacity for their first six months on the job—which frustrates peers, managers, and certainly internal and external customers. Just as employee performance quality affects the customer experience, employee turnover affects customer turnover. Customers frustrated by inexperienced sales, accounting, or support staff take their business elsewhere. Turnover of both types negatively affects profits.

Unnecessarily high levels of voluntary employee turnover potentially affect every product or service that you buy or use. Would you want to be a patient in a hospital with 55 percent voluntary employee turnover? The overstressed experienced employees would have oriented the newly hired, credentialed hospital employees, but is that enough? Would you want to buy a car manufactured by a team of cross-trainees in their first days in their new roles? Would you even want your car washed by a 100 percent "first day" crew? Would you want to be the manager in any of these situations, especially if high voluntary employee turnover were a constant part of your job? No? No wonder!

It is the manager's responsibility to develop staff and ensure that quality and productivity goals are met. Some turnover is expected and necessary, but using highly selective recruiting and following with fast assimilation, ongoing development, and good management should keep terminations for cause or lack of performance to a minimum. It should be no surprise that an edict to annually ferret out the lowest 10 percent among staff performers acts like a sword of Damocles among the remaining "keepers," with the result that mandated turnover can create unplanned, domino-effect turnover amid lower morale and productivity. More than 10 percent turnover can be disruptive and expensive because of the continual training and development needs of disproportionate numbers of new hires.

Many organizations focus on one number: the bottom line. In a time of so many job and career choices, the best managers realize that superior profits are possible only with superior customer loyalty—which comes from excellent performance from literally every employee who comes in contact with your organization's product, service, or customer. Employees who fear job loss are on the bottom of Maslow's Hierarchy: those concerned with survival needs (see figure 1). It takes more than a focus on profits to produce them. Even shareholders are beginning to communicate that fostering "survival of the fittest" employees is no way to evolve a culture that cares about customers and thus retains them. Human psychology does not work that way.

As a manager of choice, you have the power to positively affect profits for your organization by igniting the imagination, enthusiasm, productivity, and loyalty of your employees. This can translate not only into benefits for the organization, but also into benefits for your career, and much less stress for you as an individual. When organizational sales improve, every manager's job becomes easier.

When your senior management discusses the dual goals of profit and shareholder value, it can be difficult to understand how your individual actions can make a difference. Yet, research shows that your focus on people management produces profits. "Superior human capital practices . . . are a leading indicator of increased

Figure 1 Maslow's Hierarchy

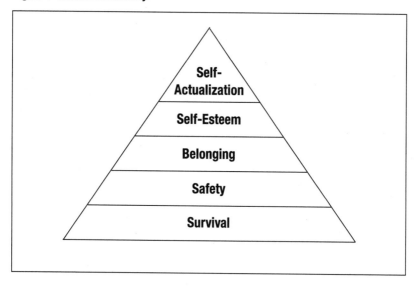

shareholder value. Superior human resources practices are a key to attraction, retention and . . . business outcomes," according to consulting firm Watson Wyatt in its report "Human Capital As a Leading Indicator of Shareholder Value."[21] Correlation of your role in employee and customer retention, productivity, and profits and shareholder results has been shown in a number of studies:

- A Bain & Company productivity study of Chicago-based advertising giant Leo Burnett reveals that a 5 percent increase in employee retention rates increases productivity by more than 20 percent and profits by 50–100 percent.[22]

- A Walker Information study featured in *Stakeholder Power* documents the turnaround of Stalcop, a once-stagnating international manufacturer of electrical, automotive, and replacement parts whose senior management was determined to make customer satisfaction and employee commitment its new marketplace differentiators.[23] After eighteen months, the percentage of employees responding that they "feel a part of the family at Stalcop" increased twenty-nine points, and customer perceptions of customer service increased thirty-two points—which increased levels of repurchasing and sales per account (customer loyalty), which increased the company's topline performance.

- Studies of a variety of product sales and service companies with high levels of employee loyalty (and retention) reveal how referrals from their loyal customers take over the function of advertising and sales. Referred customers have a $0 acquisition cost, which significantly boosts profitability year after year.[24]

- A Towers Perrin survey of U.S. employees working for publicly traded companies compares high-performing companies (those trading in the top 25 percent of the group in terms of five-year total shareholder return) with low-performing companies (those in the bottom 25 percent) from 2Q 1996 to 2Q 2001.[25] They found that "success breeds success . . . a high performing company attracts, engages and retains high performing employees whose work strengthens the company."[26]

Tying It All Together

The people management–profit link is the new financial relationship to be mastered. Study after study demonstrates that the 1–2–3 hierarchy of investors, customers, and employees needs to be reevaluated so that all three are on equal footing. It all starts with you as a manager and the role you play as an enabler of an organizational culture that encourages the recruiting and retention of top talent.

Managers of choice (MOCs) are the competitive advantage that will take organizations through mergers, acquisitions, and slower-growth economies while providing the level of quality of products and services demanded by customers with global options.

Managing well today requires addressing four employee needs:

- To be recognized as a source of unique potential and talents

- To trust and be trusted

- To be engaged with work, peers, customers, and the larger community

- To stay competitive through continuous learning

Employee turnover is not just a profit killer—it makes the daily work experience negative for peers, managers, and even customers. If employees quit their managers, not their organizations, then it stands to reason that those employees who perform above and beyond the call of duty do so because of their managers. Top talent wants to work for top managers. The quality of the manager–employee relationship is the key to mutual career growth and organizational profits.

MOCs innovate the people management process. You must empower yourself to redesign your role as well as the tools you will use and the metrics by which you are judged. Managers can transform themselves into managers of choice. They ignore the voice in their head that says, "No one ever did that for me," because they want to be better than any manager who would use negative experiences as a model.

MOCs know that people management is "job one." These talent magnets are found at every level in every type of organization and they have a long line of talented people who want to work for them. They bring out the best in their staffs by hiring the best, enabling the best, measuring the best, and rewarding the best in their employees. MOCs are the engine that powers their organization's EOC strategy to reality and profitability. They are the role models who inspire others. You can be one of them!

Discussion Questions

1. In the past three years, what demographics have changed in your geographic area? How has this change affected your challenge to recruit and retain top talent?

2. What evidence do you have that employees are becoming "consumers of the work experience"? How does this change affect your job as manager?

3. What is your department's employment brand? Is it the same or different from your organization's product or service brand? Why?

4. Have you ever worked for an MOC? Who are the MOCs in your organization? Why do their names come to mind?

5. Which of the five MOC competencies are strengths of yours? Which MOC competencies must you develop?

Resources

To learn more about the people management–profit link, read:

Competing for Talent by Nancy S. Ahlrichs. Palo Alto, CA: Davies-Black Publishing, 2000.

The Loyalty Effect by Frederick F. Reichheld with Thomas Teal, Bain & Company. Boston: Harvard Business School Press, 1996.

Stakeholder Power by Steven F. Walker and Jeffrey W. Marr. Cambridge, MA: Perseus Publishing, 2001.

The War for Talent by Ed Michaels, Helen Handfield-Jones, and Beth Axelrod. Boston: Harvard Business School Press, 2001.

Managing with Whatever It Takes (WIT)

"Management and improv require the same skills: listening without prejudgment, trusting that the group can solve a problem, and letting go of one's own needs to control situations or predetermine outcomes."

—**Izzy Gesell,** corporate trainer and motivational humorist

A new understanding about the tradeoffs for hard work is emerging. Multiple social and business influences have been at work reshaping the employee–employer relationship or contract. For years, work has imposed itself on the private lives of employees. Late hours and work taken home, trade shows, conferences and clients away from home, calls to come in early, beepers, and on-call status have required that family time be sacrificed in exchange for the promise of long-term employment. The overabundance of top talent and dearth of high-quality jobs until 1995 ensured that anyone employed did whatever was necessary to stay employed and be considered for advancement. The unwritten, unspoken contract guaranteed that hard work would pay off in continued employment and a decent retirement. If not the latter, at least the former was expected.

The bonds between employees and their organizations were loosened by the repeated violation of this long-standing psychological contract when employers began to lay off longtime employees, rewrite benefit packages, mismanage company finances so that retirement plans were in jeopardy, and require employees to be in charge of their own careers. Initially, the generation known as Veterans (born prior to 1946) and Baby Boomers (born 1946–64) accepted the changes and continued to *live to work*. They did not alter their work hours or approach to work. Gen X employees (born 1965–77), the children of the first laid-off workers, refused the contract concept altogether. After two decades of mergers, acquisitions, restructurings, outsourcing to *maquiladoras*, technology upgrades, and global sourcing, Gen Y (born 1978 and after) asked, "What contract?" Both younger generations are determined to *work to live* even if that means scaling down financial and lifestyle expectations. Today, after the shock of September 11, employees of all ages increasingly want their own individual contract.

No one expects the employer to take care of the employee today. The "new" contract is two-way, and more egalitarian or partnering in nature, as compared to the "old" contract of the past that instituted a more parent–child type of relationship. In an analysis of more than eight hundred business-related articles from trade and academic journals, Mark Roehling et al. conclude that there are "systematic differences across target employee groups in what they require and value in an employment relationship."[1]

Flexibility is key to the new contract. In exchange for employees' commitment to quality services, efficient processes, and the customer, the organization must demonstrate care about their work–life balance, efficiency at home, family, health, and interests. Employers today desire an empowered, committed workforce that makes decisions that are in the best interest of the organization. To increase the odds of that outcome, employers of choice (EOCs) offer a variety of work configurations and schedules, competitive compensation, developmental and skills training, and respectful, fair treatment. Just as your customers have stepped forward to partner with your organization to define the value of what is purchased, your employees—as consumers of the work experience—are exercising their right to design, accept, or reject a specific job, work configuration, or even an entire career.

The variation of employee preferences may be due to different career and life stages and levels within the organization such as new graduates versus managerial employees, white collar versus blue collar, and core versus peripheral employees. Other factors such as nationality, citizenship status, religion, disability, and so on may also play a role. A poll of 660 working Americans by management search firm BridgeGate, LLC, points to demographics as one of the factors that encourage loyalty.[2] In their study, 50.5 percent named factors other than money as the reason they continue to work for their current employer. These factors include

- **Flexible work schedule:** 17.3 percent of women valued it versus 11.2 percent of men

- **Benefits:** older employees valued benefits the most, including 30.1 percent of the 45–54 age bracket and 36.7 percent of those ages 55–64 compared to 23.1 percent of all respondents

- **Training opportunities:** younger employees (10.7 percent of respondents ages 18–24) were more attracted to ongoing learning versus 4.7 percent of all respondents

- **Stock options:** men were almost three times (12 percent) as likely as women (4.7 percent) to be motivated by stock options

- **Raises:** younger employees (ages 25–34) were more motivated (52.3 percent) than those in other age groups (43.2 percent) to stay for higher pay

Managing has never been easy, but it can be easier today if you do not limit your approach to the old contract, structuring all work on-site and during current work hours using your current job descriptions and headcount. Instead, look at the results desired and open your mind to new ways that technology enables tasks and projects to be bundled or unbundled. In the coming decade, never will so few do so much with so little continuous time together! You will no longer "manage by walking around." Being an MOC in the new century will instead require two kinds of wit: a sense of humor and a "whatever it takes" (WIT) approach to getting results.

In this chapter we cover the trends and demographic drivers behind the need for alternative work configurations, the variety of work and employee configurations that will be needed to get results, the role of employee involvement in success stories, and the use of communication, mentoring, and "managing up." Nothing is more difficult than gaining acceptance for new ideas. Selling new approaches and structures up and down the organization is a key part of managing with WIT—and a key part of being an MOC.

Last-Century Solutions Won't Get the Work Done

Even before 1995, the first year in which more jobs were available than qualified workers, businesses and not-for-profit organizations attempted to get more work done with fewer employees. Restructurings and layoffs required doing more with fewer people, so senior management—through midlevel and frontline supervisors— required overtime (paid, for the lucky few), frequently with the company president checking the parking lot after hours for "enough" cars. Overtime as well as taking work home and going in to the office on the weekend became the norm for anyone in management and for many staffers. Many managers had twenty, forty, or more direct reports "just lucky to have a job." Both managers and staffers delayed, shortened, or did not take earned vacations. No one could work only forty hours and not have their work ethic questioned.

Even with reengineering, the use of technology, and millions of dollars spent on consulting advice, getting the work done in a forty-hour workweek has been a severe challenge. A Bureau of Labor Statistics study found that 57 percent of those who take work home do so to catch up or keep up with their duties on the job.[3] When working more than forty hours (often, more than fifty hours) was not enough, employees responded by "becoming mean as snakes," developing stress-related illnesses, ignoring their customers' needs, calling in sick[4]—when only 32 percent were actually sick—conducting personal business on company time, or simply quitting or changing careers. Doing more with fewer employees actually turned out to be more expensive—though the costs of hiring, orienting, and training new employees and the loss of customers were often not tracked.

Endless daily overtime—even if paid—is not a sustainable approach for getting the work done. Expected overtime is one of the reasons that Gen X employees do not want to manage and younger Gen Y employees do not want to work for anyone but themselves. Of course, you have alternatives to overworking existing staff: hire more permanent staff, hire temps to handle a backlog, outsource entire functions (overseas, if necessary), and acquire companies as a way to acquire staff. While these solutions can work, the answer is actually simpler: listen to your employees. You will hear great alternatives to staffing and scheduling woes by capitalizing on the flexible work arrangements they have been seeking—and these arrangements make it easier to attract and retain top talent. Over the course of the next ten years, much of the top talent will retire, return to school for a new degree, stay home with a new child or an infirm parent, or have a medical reason for desiring an alternative work arrangement. Working full-time is not an option for many candidates classified as top talent.

Out of necessity, managing by walking around will be replaced by managing by producing results and creating relationships—a key part of managing with whatever it takes (WIT). The requirement for every employee to be on-site from 9 to 5 (or another shift) will be impossible to achieve for the reasons listed below.

Fewer Full-Time Workers Will Be Available

This will be due to the retirement of the Veteran generation and the early retirement of up to 60 percent of all Baby Boomers by 2006[5]—yet most of those will continue working in some capacity after retirement.

- Ninety-five percent of Veteran generation employees (born before 1946) who are not yet retired plan to do at least some work after retirement, according to a Harris Poll survey.[6] They enjoy challenges and learning and are open to training. Those under the age of seventy must work within parameters that allow them to continue to collect Social Security.

- Somewhere near half of Baby Boomers (born 1946–64) will keep working after they retire[7]—whether doing project-based, consulting, or part-time work in their old fields or in entirely new careers using transferable skills—and it will shake up our organizations.

- The quantity, bench strength, and age composition of the full-time workforce will change. By 2008, 23 percent of executives and managers—and one in six employees (one in five by 2025)—will be over age fifty-five.[8]

Families and Work–Life Balance Will Be an Issue for All Ages and Both Sexes

Employees—including singles, who will be in the majority—will demand the opportunity to balance work with a private life to accommodate hobbies, school, children, eldercare, and vacations. Fathers, not just mothers, are demanding dinner at home with their children, flex-time, sabbaticals, telecommuting, and other work–life balance options.[9] Even entrepreneurs, renowned for working long hours, are rediscovering the joys of family life and work-free vacations.[10] They are disconnecting from work to revive their family relationships, energy, and enthusiasm.

At the twentieth reunion of the Harvard MBA class of 1982, even the president of GE, Jeff Immelt, showed photos of family and declined to network or talk about work issues.[11] "Captains of industry" are not alone: more employees are refusing to "check in" while on vacation, too. As more time passes, focused family time will no longer be seen as an exception.

Eldercare is a growing issue for employees. Twenty-five percent of households contain a family caregiver, according to AARP. The typical caregiver is a forty-six-year-old female with her seventy-seven-year-old mother living nearby.[12] Many employees have more than one parent or in-law in need of daily assistance.

Discriminating "Consumers of the Work Experience" Will Want Customized Work Arrangements

Sought-after employees will be able to make themselves available on their own terms. Instead of trying to win the war for full-time talent, MOCs will meet organizational goals with a mix of full-time, part-time, on-site and off-site, contingent, consulting, and project talent—any way that top talent wants to configure the relationship.

- Organizations of all sizes are becoming more telecommuter-friendly; nearly one-third of firms with 100 employees or more have formal telecommuting policies. Empty cubicles will increase as telecommuters grow to 31.5 million by 2004, according to an In-Sta-MDR study.[13] Though most telecommuters live on the East or West Coast, according to the International Telework Association and Council, this trend is expected to spread rapidly to the heartland. More than two-thirds of telecommuters say they are more satisfied with this work arrangement.[14]

- Almost 30 percent of U.S. workers fall into the "contingent" categories—temps, part-timers, contractors, and on-call employees—according to the U.S. General Accounting Office.[15]

- Nine of ten part-time workers choose part-time employment, according to the Employment Policy Foundation.[16] By 2010, temporary staffing companies are expected to add 1.9 million new jobs.[17]

- Eighty-four percent of retirees who are willing to work want part-time hours. Many already have healthcare coverage, so they lack that motivator to work longer hours.[18]

- Even full-time workers want to sculpt their workdays to fit their private life. In 2001, according to the Society for Human Resource Management, 31 percent of surveyed companies let staffers work compressed schedules (such as four ten-hour days or a "5-4/9" schedule, with a week of five nine-hour days followed by a week of four nine-hour days to get a day off every other week), up from 23 percent in 1998.[19]

Managers Will Need to Use Alternative Work Arrangements As Retention Tools As the Pressure to Change Jobs Becomes Relentless
Magazine articles with titles like "Work More, Play More"[20] and cover lead-ins like "Sick of Your Job?" or "Dream Jobs" proliferate.[21] In a time of career and job choice, employees of all ages and at all levels seek job satisfaction. Meanwhile, opportunities to change jobs are everywhere: conversations with neighbors, in the mail, on billboards or the radio, or at dinner parties, church, grocery stores, and so on. Only employees who feel their job fits their life will stay with your organization, no matter what their work configuration or pay.

WIT Alternatives Boost Candidate Choice, Productivity, and Profitability

Technology has opened the door to telecommuting, nontraditional scheduling, compressed workweeks, job sharing, distance learning, virtual teams, and even managing specific functions such as software development overseas. Combined with paid-time-off (PTO) banks, "concierge" services (e.g., dry-cleaning pickup and delivery, handyman services, and other errands), and individual schedule accommodations, these alternatives represent the majority of ways that employers are attaining quality and productivity goals while simultaneously recognizing the complexity of their employees' lives.

In an ever-lengthening list of occupations, work can be accomplished by tapping into information housed centrally but accessed and manipulated from anywhere in the world. There are few jobs—other than those requiring hands-on processes—that cannot be accomplished with at least some degree of flexibility. Even hands-on jobs can often be shared or accomplished during hours other than 9 to 5, if desired. E-mail, voicemail, conference calls, videoconferencing, and electronic reporting will replace much "face time," so timeliness and "e-etiquette" will be very important. In many cases, entire projects or even entire jobs can be completed on an ongoing basis through the use of the Internet, fax and phone lines, and instant messaging, among other technologies—and teams and departments can be made up of full-time, part-time, and contingent employees ("temps"), consultants, and contractors. For example, NetCom Solutions International, Inc., a 225-employee provider of network switches and relationship services for telecom carriers and Internet service providers in Chantilly, Virginia, has two-thirds of its employees working remotely. They use software to track project status daily. Silverline Technologies Limited, a software integration services firm based in Piscataway, New Jersey, and Mumbai, India, has a network of employees in three locations in India as well as in Europe, North America, and other sites in Asia.[22]

Telecommuting, flex-time, home offices, and other adaptations to the lifestyle needs of employees and the twenty-four-hour operation of many organizations have a variety of advantages for both employees and employers. Blue-collar as well as white-collar positions can be redesigned for maximum productivity while meeting employee needs. With alternative work configurations,

- Employees report that they are happier and healthier

- Productivity increases 15–20 percent without commute time, chitchat, shift limits, or other time constraints on work hours[23]

- Employee schedule conflicts such as childcare, school meetings, eldercare, and early evening/early morning commitments can be accommodated without sacrificing an entire workday

Employers benefit from alternative work arrangements because

- Products can be developed and produced more quickly when virtual teams or individual top talent can be accessed worldwide

- Improved customer service often balances out the initial investments in telecommuting equipment (telephone, fax machine, PDA, software)

- Improved product and service quality is feasible

- Barriers to entry for competitors may be greater

- Absenteeism is reduced

- Entire offices may be eliminated or scaled down when remote support is available. Instead of an employee-to-workstation ratio of 1:1, it could be 5:1 or even 10:1. Smaller offices can save up to 55 percent on overhead costs of office space, utilities, and supplies.[24]

- Corporate tax advantages may be available to companies that allow employees to work from home in locales battling congestion, smog, limited parking, and long commutes

- Flex-time may be used as an enticement to employees and potential employees when other benefit dollars are not available

- Jobs may be saved if part-time and other arrangements can be used as alternatives to layoffs

Alternative Work Arrangement Success Stories

Employers and managers report a variety of benefits when they expand the work arrangements beyond traditional 9-to-5 boundaries:

- **Lower absenteeism.** Xerox has reduced absenteeism by 30 percent and improved morale and customer service by putting employees in charge of scheduling. At Johnson & Johnson, absenteeism among those employees who use flexible work options and family leave policies is 50 percent lower than for the general workforce. At Aetna Insurance, female employees returned to work after pregnancy 88 percent of the time when the company established a six-month maternity leave policy with flexible return-to-work options (versus 77 percent without the policy).[25]

- **Productivity improvements.** Cigna Corp. supports 9,000 telecommuters via call forwarding, home-office equipment, and technical support and training as part of its "e-worker" program. Productivity has increased as much as 15 percent and job turnover rates have been cut in half in some divisions. "Touchdown spaces" provide 250 shared workspaces when workers do come in to the office.[26]

- **Travel with less turmoil.** Ernst & Young lowered turnover and improved client satisfaction by allowing employees and managers to negotiate work–life balance agreements every six months. Travel schedules were redesigned, and a utilization committee now meets regularly to review workloads. Employees are not compelled to check e-mail or voicemail on weekends or during vacations.[27]

- **Relocation alternatives.** PricewaterhouseCoopers found that filling positions with the right people often means looking beyond their own backyard. For example, one PWC executive lives and works in Chicago two days a week and Manhattan three days a week. He also splits his time between two areas of expertise: diversity and work–life practice and the human capital practice.[28]

- **Easier recruiting.** Scimagix Inc., in San Mateo, California, uses telework as a recruiting tool. The option to telecommute two days a week is a magnet for attracting engineers.[29]

- **Fewer OT complaints.** The Communications Workers of America used collective bargaining agreements with employers to limit mandatory overtime while requiring a joint committee to oversee and monitor overtime issues.[30]

- **Multiple benefits.** In a Sussex, Wisconsin, Kraft Foods pizza plant, employees and management collaborated on a work redesign that enabled a new schedule and team system, resulting in several of the benefits listed above. Kraft benefited from improved recruiting and retention, increased production, and reduced overhead and assembly downtime. The employees reported that the more predictable work hours resulted in easier childcare and transportation—especially important for first-time job holders from welfare-to-work programs.[31]

- **Patriotic support.** IBM created an e-workplace that allows employees and those on active duty to stay connected through instant messages, online meetings, forums, and self-service human resources.[32] Reentry into the workforce is easier for returning reservists.

The following "What's Working" example describes how one company has had great success with implementing nontraditional work arrangements.

What's Working at Nokia

You don't have to manage an American R&D effort to see the transferable elements of one company's approach to innovation, productivity, talent acquisition, and better management. Nokia, the Finnish "hit factory" of cell phones, has more than 18,000 engineers, designers, and sociologists scattered globally in small teams. Small teams at multiple locations versus many teams under one roof is but one strategy to accelerate the next cellular breakthrough. Having little hierarchy has been the key to unleashing the combined creative energy of more than fifty teams of engineers. Innovations have been made without even being approved by senior managers.

"We operate the way a great jazz band plays," says Yrjö Nuevo, chief of R&D. "There is a leader, and each member is playing the same piece, but they can improvise on the theme."

Nokia's formula for back-to-back innovation:

1. Don't locate all your R&D in a single place…disperse it.

2. Keep teams small (< 50). Give a lot of power and autonomy.

3. Flatten hierarchy; stay close to your engineers.

4. Encourage engineers to generate crazy new ideas; get innovations into production with rocket speed.

5. Welcome mistakes.

Source: Paul Kaihla, "Nokia's Hit Factory," Business 2.0 (August 2002): 66. © 2002 Time, Inc. All rights reserved. Reprinted with permission.

Getting Started with Telework

Whatever your area of responsibility, you are expected to manage for innovation and excellent results within specific budget parameters. You have probably been told that you can manage your own way to get the work done. But, unless you have the stamina to deal with constant recruiting, long fill times, and soon-wasted training of new hires who leave before there can be any ROI, today you must get the work done in new ways.

Learning how to structure successful alternative work arrangements is critical whether you start with one employee who wants a different arrangement or you need to set up a blended work group or an entire virtual team, as detailed in table 2. It requires not just changes in structure, but also changes in culture. Do not expect every department or function to have the same choice of work arrangements—but expect to see an ever-widening variety available.

Employers require innovation, speed, and high-quality products and services. Employees want work–life balance, continuous learning, and opportunities to try new ideas, as well as opportunities to be rewarded and to advance without regard for their tenure or work configuration. MOCs do not shrink from the alternative work configurations that give them the only sustainable competitive edge: top talent!

There are five steps to consider when implementing an alternative work arrangement for an employee or team:

1. **Define your need for telework.** Develop a business case with the pros and cons for the employee, you, your department, and the organization. Include the business need for the change, the selection process, costs, cost savings, need for process or cultural changes, benefits for other employees, and the communication plan.

   If a specific employee has requested flex-time, determine whether the request falls under the Americans with Disabilities Act (ADA) or Family Medical Leave Act (FLMA). If so, work closely with Human Resources. If not, ask that a flex-time request form such as the one shown on page 44 be filled out and keep copies for the employee file and for Human Resources, if needed. Plan to reassess the work configuration change one to three months after initiation, unless the change is for a brief, specific time.

Table 2 Sample Alternative Work Configurations				
	Part-Time Telework (one-time, as needed, or ongoing)	**Full-Time Telework (fixed location)**	**Full-Time Telework (mobile location)**	**Virtual Teams (local, regional, national, or global)**
Work Location	Office and remote site (home, other)	Remote site (home, satellite site)	Remote site (customer sites, office, satellite site, or car)	Multiple, even global, sites
Employee Skills Required	Communication, technical skills	Communication, time management, problem solving, self-starting, technical skills, follow-through	Communication, time management, problem solving, self-starting, technical skills, follow-through	Communication, time management, problem solving, self-starting, technical skills, follow-through, team skills, collaboration
Typical Functions	Any	Many	Sales, customer service	Variety including technical resources
Technical Requirements (minimum)	Remote access to information, computer, modem, e-mail, fax machine, telephone, possibly more	24/7/365 remote access to information, computer, modem, e-mail, fax machine, telephone, possibly satellite Internet access, conference call capability	24/7/365 remote access to information and customer databases, computer, modem, e-mail, possibly satellite Internet access, fax machine, cell phone, conference call capability	24/7/365 remote access to information and databases, computer, modem, e-mail, fax machine, telephone, satellite Internet access, conference call capability
Primary Benefits	Stress management, increased productivity	Increased productivity, recruiting and retention edge	Increased productivity, increased customer satisfaction, reduced sales costs, competitive edge	Flexibility, access to talent worldwide, competitive edge
MOC Approach	Coach and manage	Coach, offer fast, flexible feedback and flexible reporting	Help define who does what, when, how; "customer is boss"; coach versus control	Coach and coordinator

Flex-Time Request

Name _____ Title _____ Dept. _____

Manager _____ Exempt: Yes____ No____ (check one)

Flexibility requested on dates _____

Explain: (include current schedule and needed change of hours and/or location)

How will this flexibility enhance your ability to perform your job?

What coverage is needed?

What work will be accomplished? Who will benefit?

How will you stay in contact with team members? Have you met with team members already to plan the transition?

Approval _____ Date _____
                        (Name and title)

2. **Design the work plan.** You or the employee(s) in question should structure the off-site work processes and define individual roles and responsibilities. Determine objectives, how decisions will be made, the type and frequency of reporting and feedback, the technology to be used, and a timeline for tasks and/or project completion. Determine how to track time (on paper or online), if desired. With the individual or the team, jointly review and refine the work plan, goals, measurement systems, and so on to ensure fair, accurate ways to measure progress and results. Give teleworkers leeway to work in a way that makes sense to them. Nonstandard work hours may actually increase productivity. Set dates to revisit the plan one to three months after initiation and then either change or reaffirm the design. Use a form such as the one shown on page 46 to preliminarily gather information to assess the success of the arrangement.

3. **Determine needed skills and competencies and identify internal and external candidates.** Team skills, problem-solving skills, versatility, and specific technical skills are frequently needed to function off-site or as a part of a virtual team. Consider assembling an off-site team with an eye to variety in their backgrounds, experiences, education, approaches, and thinking styles. Valuing differences increases the odds for innovative outcomes. But remember, working off-site is not for everyone. Not everyone who wants to work off-site can stay focused to deliver results.

4. **Develop appropriate compensation, benefits, and rewards.** While traditional workplaces typically offer base pay with annual merit raises, managing employees in alternative work arrangements may require alternative or even multiple approaches. Variable pay is frequently linked to project completion. Use peer recognition and spot rewards (cash, tickets to events, dinners for two, or other experience rewards) for completion of phases of long projects. Full or partial health and

Flex-Time Evaluation

Name_____ Title_____ Dept._____

Manager _____ Exempt: Yes____ No____ (check one)

Flexibility requested on dates _____

Explain: (recap old schedule and current flex-time arrangement including hours and/or location)

How did flex-time enhance your ability to get the work done?

Did you accomplish the original tasks for which this schedule change was made?

Were you satisfied with the arrangement? Why or why not?

How was flex-time an improvement for your supervisor, internal customer(s), external customer(s), other?

How did flex-time affect your working relationships and productivity as a team member?

Does flex-time enhance your job satisfaction? Why?

How would you improve the arrangement?

Attach any additional thoughts or comments and copy Human Resources.

welfare benefits are often available to teleworkers, but these are not usually provided to virtual teams unless members are actual employees. Specialized training or training subsidies may be provided, if needed. You may want to consider these alternative methods with Human Resources.

5. **Seek training for yourself as a telemanager.** Nothing diminishes productivity faster than uncertainty. When we feel uncertain, we have a tendency to hold on to the old ways. To speed the transition from focusing on the change to focusing on the work, make sure that your own technical skills are current. Read widely about organizations with off-site employees, join an appropriate professional organization, and seek to be mentored by managers inside and outside your organization who have experience managing telecommuters as well as virtual teams. Ask questions so that you can anticipate teleworker and on-site employee needs and begin brainstorming solutions to potential pitfalls. Consciously begin delegating instead of giving orders. Initiate new communication patterns and schedules. Squash any negative comments or innuendo about teleworker productivity unless proof is presented. Build trust among the mix of on-site and off-site team members. Very soon, managing one or more off-site employees, or a hybrid team of full-time, part-time, contingent ("temp"), and/or consultants, will be your new norm. You may even manage an entirely "virtual" team that never meets face-to-face or comes to the office.

Tips for Becoming an MOC with Teleworkers

1. **Fight your tendency to micro-manage.** We all know that not every on-site employee is productive simply because of location. Assume that virtual employees are working hard—based on their meeting participation, reports, and results.

2. **Assess the training needs of your virtual employees—and everyone else in the department.** Ensure that everyone has the

basic technology and soft skills (communications, decision making, team skills, etc.) required to make both on-site and off-site employees successful.

3. **Provide adequate technology and tech support for off-site employees.** Off-site employees need to know what resources they can count on to keep laptops and other essential equipment functioning.

4. **Keep teleworkers connected.** If your teleworkers are in the same city, schedule regular face-to-face meetings and opportunities for fun and social interaction with on-site team members. Address issues as they surface. If your teleworkers are spread out geographically, connect everyone together with regular conference calls, videoconferences, and occasional face-to-face meetings. Ask your virtual staff for their advice on enhancing long-distance relationships.

5. **Acknowledge the paradigm shift.** "Hoteling"—the random assignment of workspace—and other approaches to shared office space make many teleworkers feel uncomfortable or even unwelcome when they are in the office. Get their input to minimize their sense of being outsiders while still maximizing the opportunity to hold down office space costs. The solution could be as simple as allowing them to put their name on their workspace or door when in the office.

Mentoring Up, Down, and Peer-to-Peer

Flexible work arrangements are a proven solution to the need for top talent, but managing team members in multiple work configurations is complex. Since speed equals "best," and meeting high quality standards is assumed, the expectation that "you can have anything you want: good, cheap, and fast—pick two" has become "you can have anything you want: perfect, free, and *now*." How can

MOCs support both customer and employee needs in a fast-paced work environment? One way is by providing creative formal or informal mentors. Mentoring programs augment the overall efforts of MOCs.

As organizations become more diverse, technology becomes more pervasive, and as the work arrangements for employees become more varied, the benefits of mentoring become more important. Mentoring helps to bond mentors and mentored employees—mentees—to the organization and improve skills and performance. Not a substitute for training or performance management, and not a replacement for a manager, mentoring speeds learning and creates synergy throughout the organization by leveraging knowledge and relationships to full advantage. Who you know—and what they are willing to tell you—makes all the difference. For mentees, mentoring accelerates the development of work and political skills as well as adaptability to change. It can unlock career potential and enhance self-esteem. Mentors benefit as they develop leadership skills, keep their business skills current, and recharge their enthusiasm. Scheduling one mentoring hour a month per employee can be a way to be less "time starved" for the employee (mentee), mentor, and the MOC because of the increase of skills of the participants.

Candidates in the hiring process often ask whether a formal mentoring program is available for new hires as well as for more seasoned employees. They are interested in whether senior managers and longtime employees participate in mentoring programs. Sophisticated job candidates know that mentoring can occur up, down, or peer-to-peer to deepen relationships within the organization and substantially improve the performance of both participants. Mentoring can also be conducted outside the organization to develop a pipeline of future employees. For a business startup or even a well-known employer, new-hire mentoring can be part of a recruiting and retention strategy that speeds assimilation, builds trust, and helps all participants to withstand the accelerated change wrought by fast growth or a fast-changing marketplace. For a more mature organization, mentoring by longer-tenured employees may be used to attract and bond new Gen X or Gen Y hires to an otherwise Baby Boomer/Veteran–majority organization. Peer mentoring and mentoring up can effectively accelerate new technology and process integration.

Selecting Mentors

If your organization has no history of formal mentoring, team with HR to start a pilot program. Encourage program participation by finding ways to put the spotlight on terrific mentors and successful mentoring stories. Being a mentor should be a prestigious, voluntary activity since the only thing worse than no mentor is a bad mentor. Very quickly, mentoring will become an expectation and a key part of the culture.

Reinvent mentoring to suit the needs of your employees. Senior-level employees cannot be the only mentors, so mentoring programs should include employees at all levels at all lengths of tenure. Some companies such as Intel use a voluntary mentoring or "partnering" program as a tool to develop in-demand skills.[33] Employees at any level enter their list of top skills—anything from time management to leadership or computer languages—in a database, to be matched with the needs of other employees who fill out an Internet-based questionnaire. The "partners" enter into a contract that usually lasts six months. Intel also uses group mentoring: speed learning at its best. One mentor is matched to a group of new recruits or new managers. Instead of discussing case studies, the mentees bring real-life situations to the table for group discussion and mentor insights.

For midlevel employees, being a mentor as well as a mentee can be used as one facet of a development plan to broaden their experience. Mentoring is a skill that Gen X and Gen Y job applicants want to learn, so they can be given the opportunity to mentor interns, students of all ages, and peers—and even opportunities to "mentor up" to senior management and long-standing employees. Younger, more diverse employees flex with change, grasp the intricacies of the Internet and other technologies, approach problem solving from a fresh perspective, and can help the organization overall to deal better with diversity and change.

With the relatively low number of African Americans and Latinos in executive, administrative, and manager positions, clearly there is opportunity for career growth that can be accelerated by mentoring. Peer-to-peer mentoring programs help minority employees to feel more comfortable and excel more quickly, but mentoring across racial, ethnic, gender, age, and other lines should also be available and encouraged. Reciprocal mentoring is often an intentional or unintentional side benefit for mentoring pairs who are quite different in age, experience, ethnic background, and so on. Managers of choice are often participants in mentoring programs—as mentors and mentees.

Mentors must understand and value the roles they play— including coach, advocate, and counselor. Be sure to recognize and reward mentors—especially those in lower-paid jobs—with spot cash awards, merchandise, or gift certificates. Mentors among the hourly staff are critical to the orientation process, explanation of company policies, and the assimilation of new hires. Make it worth their while to do a good job and entry-level employee turnover will be less of an issue. In many organizations, being a mentor is part of the performance expectations of anyone with supervisory responsibilities, and performance as a mentor is a factor in the size of bonuses. All mentees benefit when more experienced employees teach them specific skills and the subtleties of communication and share the organizational stories that can speed or trip up the best of employees. The best mentors also provide insight into how the mentee is perceived by others.

Mentoring Success Strategies

Mentors often have more than one mentee. Good mentors cultivate the mentee's own gifts when they

- Share their successes and failures

- Direct developmental assignments to the mentee

- Enable discussion of difficult subjects such as gender or racial issues

- Are an advocate for the mentee

- Sensitize the mentee to political and other factors that play a role in success at work

- Hold conversations confidential unless the conversations include the discussion of harassment or discrimination, or the physical health of the mentee or other employees is in jeopardy

See how other organizations innovate with mentoring programs in "What's Working" on page 53.

Starting a Mentoring Program

No two programs are alike. A successful mentoring program does not just happen; it must be developed, formalized, publicized, monitored, tweaked—and the best mentors must be recognized and rewarded. To accelerate your organization's growth, and to create the energized learning environment needed for a sustained upward trajectory, team with Human Resources to launch a mentoring effort. If an organization-wide program is too much, start small by training volunteer mentors and mentees in your work group. Assemble a mentoring task force and follow these steps:

1. **Determine the goals of the mentoring program.** Is mentoring intended to improve new-hire retention, increase the number of minority employees who move into middle- and senior-level management positions, or be part of a fast-track development program? Are there other goals? How long should formal mentoring relationships last?

What's Working for Mentees

Mentoring programs vary in their structure. Each organization will have its own goals.

- At GM, according to Tom Thrivierge, director of talent acquisition, "Value one is integrity. Say what you mean and mean what you say." Two types of mentors help to build trust from day one. Fresh recruits are paired for up to three months with new employees with some affinity, such as coming from the same college. At three months, new hires receive a longer-term mentor. According to Thrivierge, "Mentors and supervisors at GM are focused on building relationships with new employees. Supervisors introduce the new employee to their mentor."[34]

- To help new recruits of color, Ernst & Young pairs them with partners who have requested to mentor an employee of color. Instructional courses for both mentors and mentees ensure that goals are set and full advantage of the relationship is maximized.[35]

- Innovation is the lifeblood of many organizations following layoffs or reorganizations. Mentoring the "mavericks" and "agile thinkers" is needed to protect your competitive edge: top talent. At Rockwell Automation, Corp., a Milwaukee-based company that makes power, control, and assembly systems, James O'Shaughnessy, VP and chief intellectual property counsel, stepped in as "MOM": Mentor of Mavericks. He uses praise in meetings as well as 2- to 3-day focus groups that zero in on a "big idea" to keep his mentees motivated, mentally stimulated, and productive following corporate changes.[36]

2. **Design the program to meet the goals.** To better understand the range of mentoring programs in use, gather mentoring program examples from other organizations or the resource materials listed at the end of this chapter.

3. **Select and train mentors.** Seventy percent of mentoring program failures can be attributed to lack of adequate training.[37] Mentors can be volunteers or may use mentoring as part of their own development programs, but they must understand their role and the goals of the program. They also need to value the lessons they will receive from their mentees. Remember that while many successful programs involve mentoring pairs engaged in a variety of work-related activities, it is important to reeducate mentors about avoiding sexual and other forms of harassment.

4. **Select and train mentees.** Participating as a mentee is an important part of being in charge of one's own career. Even new hires benefit from an overview of the program so that their expectations are on target with program goals. While mentees are in the driver's seat, they must be open to input, willing to learn, and able to accept the limits of how much the mentoring program can help advance their career. Explain to them that they should report any incidents of harassment to Human Resources.

5. **Plan and publicize the checkpoints for the program.** Ask HR to monitor participants' progress without overstepping confidentiality agreements—trust may take a few meetings to develop. An e-mailed mini-survey sent two months after a mentor–mentee pairing can quickly determine whether progress is being made. Are mentoring pairs meeting regularly? If not, the program coordinator can make reassignments quickly without assigning blame. What types of activities do mentoring pairs share? See "Seven Activities for Better Mentoring" on page 55 for some examples. Additionally, consider conducting an annual survey to determine whether the program is meeting overall goals.

6. **Set goals and a preliminary timetable for launching an expanded or different type of mentoring program.** Many organizations have multiple mentoring programs with different

Seven Activities for Better Mentoring

"Meetings" can occur by telephone, e-mail, videoconference, or in person. Face-to-face mentoring meetings must be more than lunch and light conversation. Depending on the hard or soft skill needs of the mentee, mentoring meetings could include a variety of purposeful activities:

- Mentees can observe their mentor's cold calls, sales calls, contract negotiations, or presentations; later, the mentor can observe the mentee's cold calls, sales calls, etc.

- Mentees can observe or participate in the development of a special project or event

- Mentees can accompany mentors to a lunch with other professionals to discuss functional or industry issues

- Mentees can attend a trade show or professional organization meeting with the mentor

- Mentees and mentors can attend a training session together and discuss it afterward

- Mentees and mentors can discuss common employee issues and policies: sexual harassment, grievance procedures, attendance, performance management, etc.

- Mentees can ask mentors to review their resumes and share tips on interviewing, culture, and so on to facilitate an internal career move

goals. Let your own organization's needs determine program expansion.

Mentoring can go far to support on-site and off-site employees in the changing workplaces—and to support the ongoing efforts of managers of choice.

Managing Up to Sell Your Ideas

Once promoted to a management position, individual achievers such as yourself often fail if they have not learned how to manage people well. Even great people managers must learn how to manage in all directions—down, horizontally, and up—to become an MOC. Your future, quality of work life, career choices, and salary increases depend on your relationship with your own manager and your ability to package your ideas in a way that fits your manager's style and preferences.

Many managers have been surprised to find themselves "crosswise" with the boss. Producing regular reports, meeting production numbers, and staying within the budget are often not enough to develop the relationship, trust, and credibility needed for you to be able to sell your ideas. Managing up involves being able to sell ideas up the organization to your boss or even higher. To do that requires manager of choice competencies: excellence in talent scouting, relationship development, trust development, skill building, and organizational brand building.

The basics of managing up are the same as for managing peers and employees:

- Develop a relationship

- Be honest and dependable

- Manage expectations

- Present well-developed plans and ideas

- Be open to feedback

- Treat the boss/peer/employee as he or she wants to be treated

You may ask, "How hard can that be?" It can be very difficult, since the first step is to develop a relationship with a peer or employee so that you can regularly get his or her attention and minimize the number of times you are presented *fait accompli* decisions that either affect you or must be implemented by you. This requires having a relationship with sufficient two-way trust that nearly any topic can be discussed. Developing this level of trust will require conscious effort, restraint, and tenacity. Trust building is discussed in more detail in chapter 7.

Develop Your Personal Brand to Sell Up

We are drawn to people we enjoy and who meet our needs. In your work environment, your record of meeting your boss's needs determines whether you are someone he or she enjoys. When you walk in the door, is your boss happy to see you? No? Is it because you habitually "delegate up"? This is the first habit to break. Then get to work repairing your personal brand (what the boss expects to experience during your regular interactions). To determine your personal brand, ask yourself (or a close colleague):

- "What makes me different?"

- "What have I done lately to stand out?"

- "What would my colleagues/customers say is my greatest strength?"

- "What is my most noteworthy personal trait?"[38]

What you hope to hear are descriptors such as *competent, reliable, cool under pressure, creative problem solver, energetic* (or at least *pleasant*), *great with customers, honest, credible,* etc. The descriptors make up your brand. They go a long way toward explaining the relationship you have with your boss and the degree to which you are able to manage up to sell your ideas, plans, changes, hires, and so on.

What Is the Boss Buying?

If you want to sell anything to anyone, you must understand your customer—in this case, your boss. You may need to sell ideas and solutions, but you must first understand what your boss wants from *you.* For example, while all bosses value time, they typically have differing needs for the amount of information and degree of relationship. Some want a lot of information on a regular basis with frequent demonstration that you have insight into their challenges, preferences, and needs. These customers want to be a partner with you. On the opposite end of the spectrum are the bosses who fax an RFP with little or no information about themselves but want your proposal faxed back by a specific deadline. These customers want information only when they ask for it, and they want no personal relationship: no calls, no questions, and no chitchat. Let's assume that the latter example is rare among senior executives since the need for communication skills increases as one moves higher in the organization. Table 3 offers strategies for selling ideas up to four different types of bosses: transaction oriented, information oriented, relationship oriented, and partnership oriented.

Chances are, you and your boss require different amounts of information and/or different types of relationships. To increase your value and to create the best possible relationship with your boss, uncover your boss's needs and then deliver! Ask questions such as the following:

- "Would you like weekly or monthly reports? What format do you prefer?"

- "How much do you want me to keep you up to date on details?"

- "Do you want me to help you to gather, analyze, and understand data?"

- "To what extent do you want me to inform you about industry trends?"

Also ask relationship questions such as

- "How important is it that my people know people in your other departments, and vice versa?"

- "To what extent do you want me to advise you?"

Table 3 Four Strategies for Selling Up to Four Types of Bosses	
If your boss is:	**Sell ideas and manage up with this approach:**
Transaction oriented (wants small amount of information, low degree of relationship)	Be brief and to the point, preferably on paper or electronically. Use only one page with a brief summary statement and bullets for benefits, costs, deadlines, and any corroborating opinions. If there is a deadline for response, be sure to include that information up front. Keep chitchat to a minimum.
Information oriented (wants large amount of information, low degree of relationship)	Be brief and to the point as above—plus add an appendix with supporting materials. Include trends, reference information, resources for more information, etc., in the appendix. Make a great deal of information available. Keep conversations on task.
Relationship oriented (wants small amount of information, high degree of relationship)	Face-to-face meetings are needed; provide several examples of why this idea will work. Ask questions to involve the manager in the planning. Follow up with a written document that is tailored to your department or organization. Use specific references. Ask about his or her family, hobbies, vacation, etc.
Partnership oriented (wants large amount of information, high degree of relationship)	Meetings should be accompanied with full documentation as described in the other three boxes. Regular face-to-face meetings should be augmented with content-rich interactions via phone, e-mail, and voicemail. Ask about his or her family, hobbies, vacation, etc.

Source: Karl J. Ahlrichs, SPHR, "Selling Ideas to an Indifferent World," in a presentation at the 55th Annual Society for Human Resources Conference in Philadelphia, 2002.

Successful managing up requires functioning as a consultant to your boss in three ways:

- Think strategically: anticipate what your boss/client would value

- Manage information: share what is useful

- Advance the relationship: increase trust and commitment

To be deemed an MOC by your staff and your managers, you must master managing up. Developing trust and rapport with your boss will make managing your employees easier because you will be able to ensure a constant flow of information up and down the organization.

Tying It All Together

Nothing stays the same in any workplace. Managing will continue to require innovation of many types. Managing with whatever it takes—WIT—includes using ethical improvisation in big and small ways every day. Humor helps, too! WIT goes beyond traditional work arrangements, configurations. and interactions.

Top talent may be available for hire only if alternative work arrangements are offered. Employees who seek balance through nontraditional work arrangements are motivated by "teamwork, senior leadership effectiveness and a climate of innovation"—not the kinds of things that characterize someone just putting in time, according to a Towers Perrin Talent Report.[39] Work–life balance programs and alternative work arrangements result in improved employee satisfaction and better business performance when you involve your employees in the work configuration solutions. Initially, changes must be incorporated into the culture of the organization with metrics to measure the successes—or the need for further development. Very quickly, multiple work configurations will become the new norm.

MOCs enthusiastically support mentoring programs—or help to get one started. Mentors augment MOCs. You can learn to manage up to facilitate communication and open opportunities for your employees throughout the organization—and for yourself!

In a good economy, profitability may simply be a product of sector hype, although good management often plays a role; but in a bad economy, profitability is clearly due to good management, and it is essential. The people management–profit link has been established. Managing with WIT is good people management.

Discussion Questions

1. What is the new employment contract at your organization? Within your own work group, what are the variations in this contract?

2. What adjustments to work configurations do you anticipate needing to make in the next six months? What will be the benefits to the organization?

3. What steps will you take to start or add a mentoring program in your organization or department?

4. If you do not currently have a mentor of your own, what steps will you take in the next thirty days to either participate in your organization's program or to independently link with a mentor? How will you ensure positive outcomes?

5. What is your personal brand? How can your personal brand be improved to enhance your ability to manage up?

Resources

To learn more about keeping top teleworker talent engaged, read:

The Virtual Corporation by William H. Davidow and Michael S. Malone. New York: HarperCollins Publishers, 1992.

Work and Rewards in the Virtual Workplace by N. Frederic Crandall and Marc J. Wallace, Jr. New York: Amacom, 1998.

To learn more about mentoring, read:

Breaking Through: The Making of Minority Executives in Corporate America by David A. Thomas and John J. Gabarro. Boston: Harvard Business School Press,1999.

Connecting with Success: How to Build a Mentoring Network to Fast-Forward Your Career by Kathleen Barton. Palo Alto, CA: Davies-Black Publishing, 2001.

Getting Started with Mentoring by Myrna Marofsky and Ann Johnson. Minneapolis: Ambassador Press, 2001.

Managers As Mentors by Chip R. Bell. San Francisco: Berrett-Koehler Publishers, 2002.

"Establish Positive Mentoring Relationships" by Andrea C. Poe. *HR* 47 (February 22, 2002). Or visit www.shrm.org/hrmagazine/articles/2002.

"Moving Forward with Reverse Mentoring" by Samuel Greengard. *Workforce* (March 2002): 15. Or visit www.workforce.com.

To learn more about managing up, contact the Center for Creative Leadership in Greensboro, NC, www.ccl.org, or read:

Leading Quietly: An Unorthodox Guide to Doing the Right Thing by Joseph L. Badarocco, Jr. Boston: Harvard Business School Press, 2002.

Leading Up: How to Lead Your Boss So You Both Win by Michael Useem. New York: Crown Publishers, 2001.

Promoting Yourself: 52 Lessons for Getting to the Top and Staying There by Hal Lancaster. New York: Simon & Schuster, 2002.

Throwing the Elephant: Zen and the Art of Managing Up by Stanley Bing. New York: HarperCollins Publishers, 2002.

Working with Emotional Intelligence by Daniel P. Goleman. New York: Bantam Doubleday Dell Publishers, 2000.

Organizational Culture: How We Do Things Around Here

"The medium is the message."

—**Marshall McLuhan,** 1964

For many employees, the work world extends no farther than ten feet from their equipment or workstation—or perhaps to the cafeteria or break area. For others, the work world is any place but the company office: sometimes a prospect or client's office, sometimes their own home office, and so on. Whether your employees deal directly with the public, have internal organizational "customers," or build products for consumers, you are the organization's cultural ambassador and teacher. The medium is the message: managers are the living, breathing embodiment of the culture of the organization. It is important that the messages you are sending are aligned with the overall corporate culture. If there is a discrepancy, your employees will do as you do, not as you say.

Culture is expressed consciously and unconsciously. It is visible and invisible. The organization's mission, vision, and values statements might be posted in every employee's workspace, but culture is also an unseen but active force in every organization's victories and failures. According to Terry Deal and Allan Kennedy in *Corporate Cultures,* "A strong culture is a system of informal rules that spell out how people are to behave most of the time. A strong culture helps people to feel better about what they do, so they are more likely to work harder."[1] Jac Fitz-enz of the Saratoga Institute describes culture as the beliefs, attitudes, and values that survive changes in senior management and even changes in product lines.[2]

Culture is taught, enmeshed in the day-to-day processes, recognized, and rewarded. Culture does not guide what employees do as a result of their job descriptions, but it is embodied in *how* they do their job. Employees' internalized understanding of the culture manifests itself in visible expressions such as attire and workspace décor as well as in their treatment of people, including words, gestures, and interactions. Some say that an organization's true culture reveals itself in what employees do and say on a routine basis when they are not supervised. Violators of cultural norms are notified, ostracized, punished, or even terminated.

To better grasp how culture affects every employee's workday, imagine your same function in each of the following sorts of organizations:

- Southwest Airlines

- An IBM partner (a technology services provider)

- A family-owned grocery with five stores city-wide

- GE

- A thousand-bed hospital

Even if your responsibilities, job description, and pay were the same, would your experience of the job be the same? No! The cultures would differ significantly. Being a training manager for GE would be very different on a day-to-day basis than being a training manager for a thousand-bed hospital. Could you "do the job" in all five settings? Probably. Would you be equally successful in all five organizations? Probably not—due to the lack of "cultural fit." Organizational culture is a critical variable in the success of individuals as well as organizations—but there is no one "best" culture.

In this chapter we focus on how managers of choice (MOCs) communicate the culture inside and outside the organization, use culture to inspire innovation and deliver profitability, and expand their capabilities and understanding of the culture through peer mentoring.

Culture Is As Managers Do

As manager, you are the medium for the message—your nonverbal and verbal communications are continually read for alignment with the organization's cultural values. Both speak louder to employees than those values merely posted on the wall. Wise managers at all levels learn to express the culture consciously as a teaching tool and as a means of maximizing the culture's effectiveness. Because culture influences employee motivation, creativity, productivity, and retention, communicating the culture and aligning activities, processes, and rewards to it are critical manager responsibilities. Plus, though culture alone does not guarantee profit, it strongly influences brand messages that either succeed or fail to attract top talent.

In chapter 1 we discussed the importance of an organization's brand—comprising its product or service brand as well as its employment brand—in attracting and keeping top talent. The organization's product/service brand tells consumers what they can expect—fast service, low price, and so on. Its employment brand tells employment candidates and candidate referral sources about the organization's culture and what it is like as a place to work. Each brand is based on reputation and what the "consumer" experiences with the organization.

Typically, job advertisements include clues about the organization's culture. The company website, intentionally or not, speaks volumes about the organization and its employment brand. The interview process, if carried out on-site, provides the prospective employee with more cultural information—as does touring the facility and talking with other employees. To lower the rate of new-hire turnover, more than qualifications for the job must be discussed.

Beyond being qualified to do a particular job, a new hire's fit with the culture plays a big role in his or her long-term success. Sharing information about the mission, vision, and values of the organization with candidates enables them to determine whether their own personal values do indeed fit. MOCs include references to how candidates, if hired, would conduct their responsibilities in a way that fits the values and culture of the organization. MOCs often ask candidates to give examples of ways in which they have exhibited desired competencies and cultural sensitivities as a way of helping them in determining that fit. Some organizations deliberately mingle their product/service and employment branding in their advertising. For example, IBM's use of life-size face shots of employees—younger, older, black, white, Hispanic, Asian, and so on—along with their job credentials, instantly telegraphs a dual message.

In chapter 1 we also discussed the importance of creativity and innovation to the future of every organization, and the emergence of the employee as a consumer of the work experience. These consumers—especially top talent—are not attracted to "professional"or "competitive" organizations, but rather to managers that truly value innovation and creativity. Candidates bond with managers, not organizations. You will need to be able to communicate to top talent why they should want to work for *you* at your organization.

Table 4 Brand Attributes Uniquely Influence Employment Outcomes		
Employment Outcomes		
Job Satisfaction	Commitment	Intent to Stay
Culture	Values	Compensation/Benefits/ Development
Values	**Culture**	Values
Compensation/Benefits/ Development	Brand Strength	**Culture**
Brand Strength		Leadership
Work Environment		Work Environment
Leadership		Brand Strength

Note: Top-to-bottom rankings of brand attribute categories indicate relative strength of relationship to outcomes, based on multiple regression analysis.

Source: "People Brand: The Employment Brand Imperative," a research study by Right Management Consultants, Inc., Philadelphia, 2001, 7. © 2001 Right Management Consultants. All rights reserved. Reprinted with permission.

If we see managers as the chief communicators of the organization's culture, the research study by Right Management Consultants as presented in table 4—which shows that statistically significant relationships between brand attributes and employment outcomes such as job satisfaction, commitment, and intent to stay are particularly useful—trumpets their importance. As shown, culture is among the top three reasons for employee job satisfaction, commitment, and intent to stay. All three outcomes are critical to creating staffs that are capable of innovation and creativity.

As the organization's culture personified, the manager has an especially important role in increasing employees' job satisfaction and the organization's success. A 2002 Conference Board study titled "Special Consumer Survey Report: Job Satisfaction on the Decline" shows an erosion of job satisfaction from 58.7 percent in 1995 to 50.5 percent today.[3] Dissatisfied employees lower overall morale, productivity, quality, and profits.

Fitz-enz links culture to profitability when he says, "Together, culture, values and strategy are the foundation of business plans. Culture drives the systems designs that influence human behavior. Behavior leads to job performance and, ultimately, the results."[4] Business author and professor Gary Hamel says that managers can build an innovation culture by replacing old ideas such as "change starts only at the top," "variety is bad," and "bigger is better" with words and actions that demonstrate that speed, variety, experimentation, and imagination are good.[5] If new products, services, and processes are part of your organization's growth strategy, you can help get your department where it needs to go! That's what MOCs do!

Managers who are hired to fit the organizational culture most easily create new systems and processes that also fit the culture as well as organizational values and strategies. If your organization has set its sights on innovation, you personally must do all in your power to encourage innovative ideas. Hamel has ten rules for making that happen, as described in "Ten Rules for Designing a Culture That Inspires Innovation" on page 69.

Notice how your role is critical to each of the ten "rules." Ask your employees to set goals—and stretch goals—for themselves and for group projects. Make sure that you and your staff are reading industry publications as well as general business publications so that you can look for business opportunities that augment what is already in place. Help your employees to understand how what they do fits into the organization's overall goals and how the organization makes a difference in the community. Ask new employees for their impressions and ideas—before they become too bonded to the new job and wonder if their thoughts might be seen as heretical. Consider asking for ideas every week along with everyone's reports. Give prizes when the ideas are especially workable or creative. Try to use as many as possible. Don't be afraid to create cross-functional task forces as stretch assignments that expose employees to new departments and new challenges. Encourage courage—and publicly thank those who try but fail. Create small but mighty (and

Ten Rules for Designing a Culture That Inspires Innovation

Rule 1: Set unreasonable expectations.

Your employees' beliefs set the upper limit on what is possible. No company outperforms its aspirations.

Rule 2: Stretch your business definition.

Too many companies define themselves by what they do rather than what they know (core competencies) and what they own (strategic assets). Look for business opportunities outside the boundaries of the business.

Rule 3: Create a cause, not a business.

Every employee wants to feel that he or she is working on something that really matters to customers and colleagues.

Rule 4: Listen to new voices.

Listen to the geographic periphery and to newcomers to the organization for innovative ideas.

Rule 5: Design an open market for ideas.

Radical ideas are the only way to create wealth, both corporately and individually.

Rule 6: Offer an open market for capital.

Too few creative ideas get funded inside organizations.

Rule 7: Open up the market for talent.

"A" people want to work on "A" opportunities, so talent must be mobile in your organization.

Rule 8: Lower the risks of experimentation.

Try new things; pilot new programs. Make small bets—many small bets.

Rule 9: Make like a cell—divide and divide.

Innovation dies and growth slows as business units grow. Be small but think big.

Rule 10: Pay your innovators well—really well.

You get what you pay for—via recognition, cash, bonuses, etc.

mighty diverse) work teams. Last, but not least, use recognition, fun, training, experiences, and other noncash means to electrify your staff's excitement about innovation.

Subcultures Can Be Productive or Toxic

The CEO determines the overall organizational culture, and cascading levels of management and organizational processes echo it. It is inevitable, however, that subcultures will emerge around functional or geographic divisions. Employees in Michigan will not dress like employees in California, for example. An operation with Muslim employees might allow extra-long lunch breaks to facilitate prayers. The challenge is to maintain one overriding organizational culture while allowing—and even appreciating—productive subcultures. It is also sometimes necessary to introduce culture change to stay competitive. Globalization, new technology, the increasing diversity of the workforce, mergers, restructurings, and the participation of customers in product and service design have driven recent culture changes in many organizations. The evolution of employees into consumers of the work experience is reshaping the cultures in many organizations. MOCs learn how to adapt cultural norms to fit their particular situation and are key players when specific cultural changes are needed.

Managers can be substantial obstacles to culture change, and they have been known to throw out entire sections of the organization's stated values or other cultural practices. When a manager refutes or ignores desired values, beliefs, and attitudes and seeks to communicate and reward the development of an alternative culture, a toxic subculture can evolve within an otherwise employer of choice (EOC) organization. An example would be a clothing store manager who says, "*I* will define customer service. If a customer is unhappy, instead of taking the initiative to solve the problem, employees should come to me first before they take any action." Since the dominant culture is service oriented and employees are empowered to "go the extra mile" on behalf of meeting or exceeding customer expectations, the manager's order to slow the process of providing customer-defined customer service would create an alternative or toxic subculture. Predictably, morale would drop, employee turnover would increase, and customer satisfaction would decline, resulting in increased customer turnover. Profitability for the manager's department would go down, possibly affecting the manager's annual bonus and opportunities for advancement.

New equipment, a great strategy, a "hip" location, even a great product or service cannot overcome the negative effects of a toxic culture or subculture. The contrast between what employees understand to be the culture as expressed in advertising, on the website, and during the interview process and the real culture expressed by the manager may be so extreme that new hires leave immediately and longtime employees revert to "malicious obedience" or even sabotage. These behaviors are hardly the precursors of needed innovation or creativity.

Ideally, cohesive messages about the culture are embedded in every communication consciously produced by the organization. That will allow the same messages to be reflected in every spoken and unspoken communication between employees—no matter what their work location—and with customers in every outlet, branch, and sales office of the organization.

Communicating Culture: Do As You Say

If, as A. Mehabrian contends in "Communication Without Words," only 45 percent of effective communication involves words only, while 55 percent stems from actions and body language, then managers trying to communicate the organization's culture ("how we do things around here") must model desired behaviors and values.[6] One of the most frequent "disconnects" occurs when managers who expect their staffs to display great customer service skills when dealing with internal or external customers fail to display those same skills in dealing with their own internal customers: their employees.

Model the Values

Whatever your corporate culture, it is your charge to model the stated values. For example, if "service is #1," and you provide great customer service to your staff, your employees are likely to

- Anticipate and understand customer wants, needs, and concerns

- Respond quickly to requests

- Be courteous and patient

- Follow through on requests

- Resolve complaints to the satisfaction of the customer

- Expend extra effort to satisfy customers

- Be an advocate for their customer's needs

- Seek recognition for their exemplary service levels

If your own manager gave you this level of attention and service, would it positively affect your stress level, energy level, or productivity?

Give to Get the Values You Seek

Following is a list of fifteen ways to successfully communicate culture and values. There are many others.

1. **Link group activities to the organization's tagline.** If your organization's tagline is, for example, "Go further, faster," you might put it on department shirts to be given away at a meeting to celebrate a group achievement; build it into a department screensaver; ask employees to help develop criteria for a peer-to-peer award for employees who embody its sentiments; or use it to name a contest of department teams racing to clear out a backlog of work, etc.

2. **Print up "values" brochures, wallet cards, and posters.** Be sure to display these items highlighting the organization's values

yourself and make them available to all employees. Keep extras on hand for future hires, project staff, telecommuters, and consultants on your team. Everyone needs to know what the organization stands for.

3. **Keep scrapbooks.** Create a scrapbook of department events that spotlight individuals and teams that embody the organization's cultural values. Display the scrapbook for visitors, potential hires, and employees.

4. **Hold contests.** With input from staff, develop at least three contests a year that link employees to cultural values. Publicize winners in company media. Find ways for teleworkers or other off-site employees to participate.

5. **Document work stories.** Solicit documentation of examples of employees and management "living the values." Ask employees to tell their stories during orientation, as part of celebrating anniversaries, etc. Include the stories in the appropriate personnel files and as a part of internal resumes. As appropriate, use the stories as the basis for awards applications (see #10).

6. **Energize employee orientation.** Augment standard intranet or print materials used to communicate organizational values with stories from management and employees, and/or quizzes with prizes for new hires who can answer questions about how values are expressed in the organization. Managers could tell the company story in a way that links directly to the values. Some organizations ask new hires to develop skits, poems, or songs about one or more values as a way to imprint the culture from day one.

7. **Reinforce culture and values at meetings.** Ask staff to share one quick example of "values in action" that they have witnessed or experienced since the previous meeting.

8. **Publish a newsletter.** Ask staff members to be volunteer reporters for the organization's online and print newsletters.

Ensure that your department and employees are regularly featured by providing values-related themes and ideas for articles. Congratulate "values" contest winners (see #4), highlight "living the values" stories, etc. Use the newsletter to praise employees and provide photos whenever possible.

9. **Extend kudos on e-mail and intranet.** Use electronic communication to solicit, compile, and distribute "kudos" messages from around the organization to individual employees. Post kudos as well as upcoming events and employee/organizational news on a weekly basis so that employees are not swamped with e-mail or feel they must check intranet sites daily.

10. **Reward and recognize employees.** Create programs that reward employees who "live the values," possibly with different programs for different values. Recognize desired behaviors at least quarterly—preferably monthly—and consider creating on-the-spot awards as appropriate. At ONEX, Inc., a high-tech solutions firm based in Indianapolis, community service and customer service were cornerstones of the stated culture—employees were rewarded for community service with ONEX ("one-to-the-X-potential") pins for taking themselves, their company, and their community to the "next level." They also received "MVP" pins for customer service above and beyond customer expectations (based on letters from customers detailing the service). Repeat MVPs received pin embellishments that designated them MVP 3s or MVP 7s, etc.

11. **Manage performance.** Depending on their specific responsibilities, every employee has the opportunity to "live the values" in his or her job. At goal-setting time, jointly outline how the employee can best express the organization's values on a daily basis. Tie a percentage of bonus pay to achievement of this goal.

Encourage the employee to keep a file of examples ("kudos" e-mails, contest participation, mentoring, etc.).

12. **Put "values" in training.** MOCs often lead formal training sessions and may also tuck learning and mini-training sessions into group and one-on-one meetings. Even in technical skills training, MOCs weave in discussions about values.

13. **Conduct employee mini-surveys.** Twice a year, ask employees for anonymous feedback about your own "values in action" and their read on the department's and the company's success in living those values. Ask for new ideas to strengthen employee buy-in and utilization. Share the results with the staff and implement as many ideas as possible.

14. **Connect on-site and off-site employees.** Encourage socializing and relationship development among all employees. Consider providing inexpensive computer-mounted cameras so that faces and voices can be connected. Ask all employees for more ideas.

15. **Schedule face-to-face time.** Meet with each employee at least once a month, if not weekly. Everyone eats, so meet for breakfast or lunch, preferably off-site where you can give 100 percent of your attention to the employee, telecommuter, project staffer, etc. Alternatively, use Mondays or Tuesdays for 30- to 60-minute standing weekly meetings with each staffer. Schedules, goals, and accomplishments can be e-mailed in advance so that the meetings can be used to focus on relationship development, the individual, his or her success in the organization, and how you can help him or her to stay inspired. At every meeting, ask the "Big Three" questions:

• "How are *you?*"

• "How is the team doing?"

• "How can I help you to do a better job?"

Spotlighting the Culture via Awards

Awards build pride, loyalty, reputations, and your fan club! Building and spreading an EOC reputation is not the sole responsibility of the Marketing Communications department! MOCs keep their eyes open for awards that apply to the organization overall and for various departments, including their own. This brings the concept of "catch someone doing something right" to the next step: put the spotlight on "winners" so that other employees will emulate them—and prospective hires will want to work with them!

Organizational and individual awards help with both recruiting and retention efforts because they spotlight your organization's culture—that is, what it is like to work for your organization—and your staff will echo the statements inside and outside the walls. Finding awards can take a little time online or may be uncovered through professional organizations, journals, and business publications. Examples are listed below.

Organizational Awards

When your organization wins an award, top talent responds with resumes. Your clients, vendors, bankers, recruiters, and the community at large take notice. The response is overwhelmingly positive—and worth the effort of applying. Following is a list of some of the awards available.

- **100 Best Companies to Work For.** Sponsored by the Great Place to Work® Institute in *Fortune* magazine. February deadline. See www.greatplacetowork.com and www.fortune.com.

- **Most Admired Companies.** Sponsored by the Hay Group in *Fortune* magazine. See www.fortune.com.

- **100 Best Companies for Working Mothers.** Sponsored by *Working Mother* magazine. March deadline. See www.workingmother.com.

- **Top 25 Companies for Executive Women.** For Fortune 1000 companies only. Sponsored by *Executive Female* magazine and NAFE. See www.nafe.com or www.workingwoman.com/corp/top_25_2002.shtml.

- **Best Companies for Women of Color.** New in 2003. Sponsored by *Working Mother* magazine. See www.workingmother.com.

- **Best Companies for Workers over 50.** Sponsored by AARP. See www.aarp.com.

- **American Business Ethics Award.** Sponsored by the Society of Financial Service Professionals (SFSP). April deadline. Local awards roll up to national awards. Contact your local chapter of SFSP.

- **Wharton-Infosys Business Transformation Awards.** Global organizations with revenues of $1 billion and above. Sponsored by Infosys Technologies and the William and Phyllis Mack Center for Technological Innovation at the Wharton School of the University of Pennsylvania. April deadline. See www.infy.com/wibta.

- **School-to-Work Award.** Sponsored by the Society for Human Resource Management. September deadline. See www.shrm.org.

- *100 Best Stocks You Can Buy in [year]* by John Slatter, author and investment advisor. Hardcover book published annually in January. See www.amazon.com or contact the publisher, Adams Media Corporation.

- *The 100 Best Stocks to Own in America* by Gene Walden. Softcover book published annually in September. See www.amazon.com or contact the publisher, Dearborn Trade.

- **"Investments That Pay and Pay,"** in *Investing Kiplinger's.* September nomination deadline. See www.kiplinger.com.

- **The Principal 10 Best Companies for Employee Financial Security.** Sponsored by The Principal Financial Group. February deadline. See www.principal.com.

- **Best Websites for Diversity.** Sponsored by www.DiversityInc.com.

- **Employer Support Freedom Awards.** Sponsored by the Employer Support of Guard & Reserve (ESGR). See www.esgr.org.

- **The Secretary of Defense Freedom Awards.** Sponsored by the Employer Support of Guard & Reserve (ESGR). See www.esgr.org.

- **Company That Cares.** Sponsored by United Way. Contact your local United Way office.

- **NMSDC Corporation of the Year.** Sponsored by the National Minority Supplier Development Council (NMSDC). See www. nmsdc.org or call 212-944-2430.

Departmental or Individual Awards

Being nominated for one's work as an individual or for the quality of one's department is a unique thrill. If you believe that your department qualifies, or that one of your colleagues deserves an award, team with your Marketing department to get the nomination in by the deadline. Missed it this year? Mark your calendar well in advance for next year! Start a trend within your organization to set your sights on being bona fide winners of awards such as the following:

- **Award for Professional Excellence.** Sponsored by the Society for Human Resource Management (SHRM). March deadline. See www.shrm.org.

- **Award for Professional Excellence.** Sponsored by your local chapter of the Society for Human Resource Management. June deadline. Check your local SHRM chapter website.

- **SHRM Innovative Practice Award.** Sponsored by the Society for Human Resource Management. December deadline. See www.shrm.org.

- **Volunteer of the Year Award.** Sponsored by your local chapter of the Society for Human Resource Management. June deadline. Check your local SHRM chapter website.

- **CFO Excellence Awards.** Sponsored by *CFO* magazine. See www.cfo.com.

- **Best Place to Work for Finance Professionals.** Sponsored by *CFO* magazine. April deadline. See www.cfo.com.

- **100 Best Places to Work in IT.** Sponsored by *ComputerWorld* magazine. January deadline. See www.computerworld.com.

- **Top 10 Best Places to Work in IT for Benefits.** Sponsored by *ComputerWorld* magazine. March deadline. See www.computer world.com.

- **Premier 100 IT Leaders.** Sponsored by *ComputerWorld* magazine. March deadline. See www.premier100.com.

- **Silver Anvil Award or Bronze Anvil Award.** Sponsored by the Public Relations Society of America (PRSA). March deadline. See www.prsa.org.

- **My Boss Is a Patriot Award.** Sponsored by the Employer Support of Guard & Reserve (ESGR). No deadline. See www.esgr.org.

- **NMSDC Leadership Award.** Sponsored by the National Minority Supplier Development Council (NMSDC). See www.nmsdc.org or call 212-944-2430.

Many more local, regional, and national awards exist. Partner with your Marketing or Human Resources department to pursue them. It will be well worth the time and effort. When job candidates and candidate referral sources know about your organization's award-winning culture and employment brand, your job becomes easier. And, your current employees will receive positive feedback for working for an award-winning employer, have more pride in their job, and develop the stamina for the tough times. Awards bond employees to the organization.

Don't Be Lonely in the Middle: Create an MOC Community

They say it's lonely at the top. As a manager, you know that it can be lonely in the middle, too. To augment and support existing MOC efforts, individual managers (this means you!) must create mechanisms for managing better and to create 360-degree support for all those striving to become MOCs, not just the "high-potential" candidates. You need an MOC community.

Managing is not like math: there is more than one "correct" answer. The array of staff issues and potential solutions can seem endless. Collaborating with other managers on a regular basis is often the fastest, most satisfying way to grow your own people management skills as well as the collective wisdom of all involved managers. Creating an MOC community results in a cross-departmental, cross-functional network of friendships, communication, trust, and cooperation during good times and bad, as shown in "What's Working" on page 81. An MOC community speeds organizational alignment with new initiatives. Who you know does matter! Knowledge of others around the organization can open up career options and facilitate the career movement of management and nonmanagement employees within the organization so that they do not leave due to limited options. Building and maintaining alliances throughout the organization is a critical ingredient for the smooth functioning of the organization overall.

According to VECTREN's Kathy Humphrey, general manager and director, Government Relations,

> The quarterly meetings speed the overall accomplishment of business. At the Leadership Forum meetings, we get to hear more

What's Working at VECTREN

VECTREN Corporation, a 2,000-employee energy and applied technology holding company based in Evansville, Indiana, is the result of the merger of equals: Indiana Energy, Inc., SIGCORP, and Dayton Power and Light. From day one, Chairman Niel Ellerbrook championed the strategy to become an employer of choice and develop a "culture of possibility" to set VECTREN apart from other utilities and employers, as well as to build trust, credibility, and communication among its geographically dispersed employees.

To uniformly communicate the overall employer of choice strategy of the company, the chairman hosts two quarterly meetings for two management communities: the Leadership Forum for all fifty corporate officers and directors, and the Manager Forum for approximately one hundred next-level managers from across Indiana and in Dayton. Four times a year, the groups meet over two days to focus on strategic alignment, personal development, and leadership development. Each quarter, one of the four core values takes center stage: capital (return on investment), community (corporate citizenship), customers (customer satisfaction), or colleagues (valuing diversity). Over three years, the ownership of the quarterly meetings has shifted from senior management to a cross-functional team that strives to involve the attendees in experiential learning to deepen their commitment to, and knowledge of, the organization and each other.

in-depth information from the experts in every area and have the opportunity to ask questions and have discussions so that the entire group can understand complex business issues outside of each of our areas of expertise.

As someone located in Indianapolis, I find that e-mail and voicemail cannot replace the effectiveness of actually meeting someone and talking in person. In a fast-paced, geographically dispersed organization like VECTREN, separation by even floors in the same building can be barriers to relationship development and communication. These meetings provide an opportunity to communicate simultaneously with every business unit in the company and quickly gain their support for a variety of initiatives. One of the greatest benefits, however, is the opportunity to talk before the meeting and during the breaks. An astonishing amount of business can be moved forward or even completed through face-to-face conversations.

MOC communities are dynamic and should change to meet the evolving needs of the participants. At VECTREN, the MOC community has changed over time to connect lower levels of management together across the company, as well as to bring together multiple levels of management that otherwise might not have the opportunity to meet due to distance or area of specialty.

Whether you are in a large or small organization, you can take the initiative to create an MOC community. It will reinforce your organization's culture and support you in your individual development. As appropriate, initiate at least one of the following:

- **An informal MOC mentors group.** Mentor each other in a group setting. All you need are six to twelve other managers, a meeting place, and an egg timer. The best groups require no minutes, no dues, no sponsors, and no committees. Consider standing meetings every other week. Typically, three-quarters of the members will attend each meeting. The small group size combined with a structured format for the meetings is crucial for success.

  At the first meeting, determine time and frequency of future meetings as well as a list of topics or development needs for the group. Narrow and prioritize the list. Each member should volunteer to research one topic in terms of approaches and options being used at other organizations and commit to a presentation date. In addition, the group members can serve as a board of directors for each other.

Table 5 Flip-Chart Sign-in Sheet for the Informal Mentoring Group			
(Example)	**Since the last meeting, rate your:**		
Name	**Progress on past issues (1–10) (1 = low, 10 = high)**	**Physical/psychological well-being (1–10) (1 = low, 10 = high)**	**Workload and accomplishments (1–10) (1 = negative, 10 = positive)**
Sally DiNatale	8	8/6	3/7
Jan Goldbach	5	8/6	4/8
Roger Bain	10	7/9	5/9
Mel Middleton	7	8/8	4/8
Etc.			

The meeting should always begin on time. Begin each meeting with brief, informal socializing to allow everyone to arrive and to facilitate discussion about the outcomes of issues presented at previous meetings. Find ways to incorporate fun into these meetings. Refreshments are optional. Have everyone sign in and rate their progress on issues, physical and psychological well-being, and workload or accomplishments on a flip-chart. An example is shown in table 5.

Sitting around a conference table, on which sits a three-minute egg timer, members are charged individually with developing a succinct description of a problem. The range of issues covered in one meeting might include two employees engaged in conflict, the need to find a specialty healthcare center for an ailing in-law, an accounts receivable challenge, the need to close three pieces of business by month-end, queries about the quality of service provided by specialty consultants, discussion of the best MBA programs, and so on. Members may decide to delay important decisions until the next meeting of their peer mentors.

Once each manager's issue is described, peer mentors should take no more than five minutes total to offer rapid-fire solutions and alternatives. Each member is responsible for writing down the suggested approaches. Very quickly—in no more than eight minutes total per manager—the spotlight moves around the room. Each member receives high-quality mentoring and also learns from the issues and proposed solutions of others! In the last twenty minutes of the meeting, a brief presentation is made of that meeting's topic, references and resources are shared, and a discussion follows. At the end of each meeting, a different member could share an inspirational quote from a successful business leader.

- **A formal managers mentoring program.** Coordinate with Human Resources to create a peer mentoring program for MOCs. Refer to the list of resources at the end of this chapter and contact peers at other organizations for ideas. The mentoring program should be designed to complement any existing mentoring programs, other leadership development efforts, and the culture. Your Human Resources partner can research and source assessments to identify gaps in needed capabilities and pair managers for the purpose of developing needed skills through activities, research, and discussion. A small task force should design training for both mentors and mentees. MOCs can play either role with different colleagues.

- **A quarterly leadership forum for managers.** In cooperation with HR and Training, tie content to the achievement of strategic goals. Volunteer to be on the cross-functional task force to design and coordinate the meetings.

- **An MOC book club and book exchange.** Meet monthly to discuss a book or concept agreed to previously. Buy books in bulk at reduced rates from local bookstores, the publisher, or online sources such as www.amazon.com or www.half.com. When starting the club, create an initial reading list that addresses organizational or level-specific issues. Solicit or assign volunteers to lead discussions and help managers to determine how to put lessons to work in their areas. Consider compiling an MOC reading list and library for other managers to use. Ask your organization to fund the book buying to encourage greater participation. Per-person costs could be limited to $150–$200 per year. Hold meetings using a "BYOBB" (bring your own book and breakfast) or brown-bag lunch format. Ask each participant to commit to a specific action at the end of the meeting.

- **An MOC retreat.** To deepen relationships and provide a day away to focus on strategic issues, plan an off-site retreat for middle and frontline managers. Ask Human Resources or Organization Development to determine the agenda by surveying the potential attendees. Set reasonable goals and be sure to incorporate fun. Secure senior management participation for part of the day plus an outside presenter or facilitator. In advance of the retreat, schedule your own departmental or functional meetings to be able to share plans, challenges, information, and so on.

- **MOC recognition programs.** Peers know who are the best among them. As a natural next step in creating an MOC community, develop recognition programs and ask members to determine criteria, frequency, nomination process, and even prizes. Publicize the winners.

- **External MOC awards.** In conjunction with Human Resources, Marketing, or Corporate Communications, enhance your organization's service, product, and employment brands and showcase effective managers through external awards such as those described earlier in this chapter.

Tying It All Together

MOCs know that a strong culture enables their staffs to successfully tackle big challenges. MOCs bond with each other—and their employees bond with the organization—through shared experiences, shared values, and a sense that they are part of something special. MOCs champion recognition programs that reinforce individuals and teams to further strengthen the culture. They create communities so that a sense of "we" is built on mutual understanding and respect. They know that the medium is the message: managers are the culture personified.

Discussion Questions

1. What would your employees say are the values you consciously communicate on a regular basis? Which organizational values do you need to communicate better?

2. Are there organizational values that are difficult for you to communicate? Why?

3. Do you know of organizational, functional, departmental, or individual awards that you could share with your Marketing, Corporate Communications, or Human Resources departments? How can you team with them to send in a winning application?

4. Pick an organizational value that you believe is critical to your department's productivity. How can you involve your employees in designing a reward and recognition program for that value?

5. Which managers are currently mentors to you? How can you deepen the relationships by offering assistance to them? If you do not have an informal peer mentor, set up three lunch or breakfast meetings to uncover a potential mentoring relationship.

Resources

To learn more about the role of managers and the power of organizational culture, read:

Corporate Cultures by Terry Deal and Allan Kennedy. Reading, MA: Addison-Wesley, 1982.

The 8 Practices of Exceptional Companies by Jac Fitz-enz. New York: Amacom, 1997.

The Gifted Boss by Dale Dauten. New York: William Morrow and Company, 1999.

Seven Zones for Leadership by Robert Terry. Palo Alto, CA: Davies-Black Publishing, 2001.

To learn more about creating an organization-wide MOC community, read:

Community at Work: Creating and Celebrating Community in Organization Life by Patricia K. Felkins. Cresskill, NJ: Hampton Press Communication Series, 2002.

The Membership Organization: Achieving Top Performance Through the New Workplace Community by Jane Galloway Seiling. Palo Alto, CA: Davies-Black Publishing, 1997.

The New Managerial Mentor: Becoming a Learning Leader to Build Communities of Purpose by Patricia J. Fritts. Palo Alto, CA: Davies-Black Publishing, 2001.

Management Metrics
That Matter

"Experience is the critical source of value for consumers."

—C. K. Prahalad and V. Ramaswamy,

"The Co-Creation Connection"[1]

People management is the new organizational core competency for your competitors, so it must also become your core competency. Excellence in people management is the value proposition that you must bring to your organization, because employees have long valued their managers' "soft" skills. Employees reward their personal manager by gladly returning day after day or project after project to meet ever-increasing goals. They so value the experience of working with their manager that they hang in during tough times. If they do not value the experience of working with their manager, they punish him or her in one of two ways: (1) by doing the minimum and virtually "quitting on the job," or (2) by voting with their feet and leaving the organization. Traditional manager performance metrics—"get your reports in on time and meet budget/production/sales goals"—look at outcomes but do not measure the people management successes that lead to meeting strategic goals. This is a disconnect.

Like all employees, you do what you are rewarded for doing and you do what is measured. Since getting work done well will require managing with whatever it takes (WIT), your staff will increasingly be a mosaic of not only diverse employees, but also employees with diverse work arrangements: full-time and part-time workers, teleworkers, virtual teams, project staff, consultants, and so on. It is important to manage each member of your staff well—no matter how his or her diversity presents itself. You and your organization will be rewarded if your individual performance goals and development plan keep you focused on the essential metrics of people management. Only then will your staff deliver consistent performance in this era of open career and job choice. Your people management skills determine whether your employees choose to deliver their best efforts to you, your department's work, and your organization.

Though pharmaceutical companies are sometimes singled out in their quest for speedy development of new products and services—while exceeding quality and efficiency targets—every organization today has an innovation mandate. The "100 Best Companies to Work For"—probably the nation's top employers of choice (EOCs)—have long recognized people management as the foundation of innovation, quality, and long-term profits. Managers at EOC organizations use targeted performance management tools, developmental approaches, and metrics to ensure that their managers have the needed information to guide their individual performance management, skill and competency development, and their day-to-day decision making and prioritizing.

In too many organizations, strategic goals are missed because only employees—but not managers—must align their performance goals to the larger strategy. Managers spend days and weeks preparing useful performance management feedback for their employees but receive reviews themselves that are perfunctory at best or often omitted altogether. If your organization's management performance development system does not align with new organizational goals, it is up to you to get the ball rolling with a conversation with your HR department, or your own manager.

When done well, performance management builds the relationship between the employee (in this case, a manager—you!) and the supervisor (your manager) and the larger organization. Performance management systems should recognize excellence, build on strengths, and provide development plans to build new skills or correct deficiencies. Whether for employees or for those in management, the expectations bar is being raised. (The five main competencies now needed to manage—talent scouting, relationship building, trust building, skill building, and organization brand building—are described in depth in part 2.)

New metrics are needed to put the focus on the activities that ensure quality hires, faster assimilation, staff development, internal career movement, and higher retention rates for top talent. The new measurements may uncover a need for managers to learn new skills or to use different competencies, but these new skills and competencies will position them for positive career movement. In this chapter we see how MOCs are redefining and aligning their performance management goals and metrics to the strategic goals of the organization.

What Manager Metrics Matter?

As a manager, you know that inspiring productivity, creativity, and innovation among your staff requires more than a single-minded focus on achieving budget numbers—whether those numbers are production quotas, sales goals, or spending limits. Too often in your meetings with senior management, however, production, sales, or spending are the only measures that are discussed. To enhance your own ability to reach production, sales, or other financial goals, start gathering additional metrics that lead to the attainment of your organization's strategic goals.

If you are a member of a professional peer group and know managers at other organizations who are known for terrific people management practices, ask to benchmark their performance management metrics informally. If you do not have contacts at other organizations, you can still take action to improve your organization's metrics and performance management processes.

Work backwards from your ultimate goals to determine the types of actions that must occur (how frequently and at what quality level) to enable the desired outcome. For example, sales reps will analyze the number of committees and professional organizations they must join to develop the relationships needed to give them the pool of appropriate prospects required to get a sufficient number of requests for sales appointments granted. Then they determine the number of sales calls needed to get a request for proposal, number of proposals needed to close a sale, number of sales needed before a "big one" comes along, and so on. Start your own "backwards analysis" to develop the metrics that matter in your area. You can share the information with your HR department or your manager to consider as processes are reviewed and updated in your organization.

You control many elements of attracting and retaining top talent. You also control overall departmental and organizational goal achievement. Your charge is to track metrics that identify current as well as developing problems so that you can take quick action. Metrics that matter provide immediately useful information that can be compared monthly, quarterly, and year-to-year as well as among departments. To develop useful metrics, focus on the activities that inspire commitment to the organization and develop and retain your current top talent. Track a baseline six months or one year and then commit to improvements.

Measure Employees As True Assets

Whether your staff is made up of full-time employees only or a mosaic of full-time and part-time workers, teleworkers, project staff, consultants, and so on, three types of people management metrics should be considered for tracking: retention, staff development, and recruiting and assimilation. Following is an expanded list of metrics under those three headings, along with suggested goals. Determine your baseline results and set meaningful goals for improvement.

Retention Metrics and Goals

- Percentage of your employees participating in annual training: 100 percent

- Percentage of your employees receiving formal mentoring (if available): 100 percent

- Percentage of your employees who receive departmental or organizational awards for achieving performance or values goals: 50 percent or more

- Percentage of your employees who qualify for spot awards and/or are recognized in the organization's newsletter: 50 percent or more

- Percentage of your employees who contribute ideas for cost savings and/or names of potential clients or vendors: 100 percent

- Percentage of your employees who refer at least one qualified job candidate a year for any position in the organization: 100 percent

- Percentage of your employees who have taken advantage of "open door" access to you (face-to-face or online): 100 percent

- Percentage of your staff's events you have attended: 80 percent or more

- Percentage of turnover of your top 25 percent of employees (top talent): 5 percent

- Percentage of your employees who name you as their reason for leaving: 0 percent

- Top three reasons that your employees leave (from exit interviews)

- Percentage of your employees who provide input for your performance review: 50 percent or more

- Number of nominations for manager or mentor awards from your peers and/or employees (if available): 1 or more

- Percentage of voluntary turnover per month: < 10 percent annualized

Staff Development Metrics and Goals

- Time to acceptable productivity: days, weeks, or months; the goal varies by position

- Performance level of your new hires 6–12 months after hire: 25 percent of new hires above overall group's average performance

- Percentage of your employees who receive both technical and soft skills training annually: 100 percent

- Percentage of your employees given "stretch" assignments or serving on cross-functional task forces: 50 percent or more

- Percentage of your employees or employees from different departments promoted to fill your department's openings: 50 percent or more

- Percentage of your employees reviewed by their anniversary date or by other organizational deadlines: 100 percent

Recruiting and Assimilation Metrics and Goals

- Time to fill positions from requisition to start date: 30 days for entry-level positions to 4–6 months for management positions

- Time from candidate's first contact (or HR's first contact with you about candidate availability) to interview: 1–5 days maximum, fastest for highest-demand candidates

- Percentage of diversity hires: 10 percent or more

- Percentage of new hires who attend formal orientation: 100 percent

- Percentage of "bad" hires who are terminated or quit within 12 months: calculate your organization's average new-hire turnover and strive to bring it lower every quarter; the national average is up to 25 percent

360-Degree Manager Performance Management

Top-down, performance management processes performed by a single person can be demotivating as well as counterproductive for managers and employees because the person in the manager's role for the review may see only reports and have little day-to-day contact with the substance or delivery of the employee's work outputs. One of the most useful alternatives you have is multi-rater, or 360-degree, feedback from your manager, peers, and employees; no matter what their work status, they are all your internal "customers." Many organizations use a 360-degree review that focuses on the manager's performance alignment with overall organizational goals (senior management's definition of value) as well as people management skills (employees' definition of value).

The multiple raters—your peers, employees, managers, or others—can anonymously complete the performance assessment process on paper or online, often in less than twenty-five minutes.

You can also rate yourself and then compare your self-rating with ratings from others. The assessment should include questions that determine how well you model the stated organizational values to your employees. This is a critical element of trust building that will be discussed in depth in chapter 7.

Consumers expect the opportunity to provide feedback, whether they are diners in a restaurant, purchasers of a car, or consumers of the work experience (employees). A request for employee feedback sends a clear message that senior management values employee input. Asking employees to provide feedback is a key to developing individual relationships with your employees and developing team relationships among them. Learning to listen and respond appropriately to their feedback is part of your own self-development. Your employees will watch and listen to your responses, and in turn learn how to accept and better use feedback.

Multi-rater performance management tools are the natural next step in an organization that has established open, up-and-down communication channels. In contrast to top-down appraisals, multi-rater input is more easily accepted by the person being rated, can lead to more consistent manager development, and helps to align individual goals with corporate goals. Many online 360-degree tools provide development plans that correspond to specific management competency development needs, or you and your manager (with HR's assistance) can design specific development exercises. Results from 360-degree appraisals can be compared year-to-year to determine the effectiveness of the most recent development plan and to set new development goals.

Aligning your performance development with the organization's current strategic goals requires more than budget adherence. By taking the initiative to help make needed changes, you send the message that accountability for living the organization's values and culture is not just for lower-level staff. If your organization needs updated performance development and performance management for its managers, approach Human Resources (or even your own manager) with the metrics that you believe will both drive and measure your department's productivity.

Why Change Current Performance Management Measures?

Turnover of employees at any level is expensive by itself—and high turnover can have a significant negative effect on goal attainment for specific departments, business units, and the entire organization. At a time when organizational goal achievement will depend not just on full-time employees and part-time staff, but also on your ability to locate, hire, and repeatedly rehire teleworkers, project staff, and consultants, your people management skills are essential. Speed to hire will be considerably enhanced if ex-employees and past project staff will return in some capacity or will refer other candidates. Shorter fill times are one of many benefits when your own performance management measures are updated to include 360-degree input from others. With access to relevant data, you can adjust your own performance to turn down turnover rates as in the "What's Working" example on page 98.

In *Competing for Talent*, the costs of turnover were established from a variety of sources including compensation consulting firms and professional organizations.[2] Current estimates remain steady, from between four to five times annual compensation if there is turnover of an experienced sales representative, to one and one-half times annual compensation for exempt employees, to half a year's wages for nonexempt workers. The costs add up quickly. In any organization, the loss of top talent can lead to significantly more employee turnover, increase employee and manager stress, destroy teamwork, delay projects, increase customer turnover, and reduce profits.

To calculate the cost of turnover for one person in your department, consider the typically ignored "blue money," or lost productivity and time for supervisors, peers, and subordinates, as well as the more easily tracked "green money," or budgeted costs such as

What's Working at Wal-Mart

Wal-Mart store managers get a "People P & L Statement" every two weeks along with their other regular financial updates. The reports allow managers to compare monthly rolling turnover rates for the whole company with their own store. The report scrutinizes the timeliness of performance appraisals, the amount of training and orientation completed, records of promotions, and other retention factors. Result: instead of losing nearly half of all new hires within ninety days, turnover is down 25 percent in some markets, and trends suggest that further declines are to be expected.[3] Wal-Mart is on *Fortune*'s "100 Best Companies to Work For" list.

recruitment advertising or drug testing (see the form on pages 100–101). If the cost of replacing just one person is eye-opening, the cost of your entire department turnover over the course of a year will leave you breathless. This is a source of hidden budget dollars that can and should be spent on activities that magnify retention and productivity.

Employers of choice (EOCs) have high standards that attract employees with high standards. Chances are, you were originally attracted to your organization because its brand matched your own personal expectations. If your organization tracks employee turnover by manager, you have a strong positive indication that senior management knows the important role that frontline and middle managers play in organizational profits. Profits are the ultimate outcome of a chain of positive people management events throughout an organization. Creating an EOC organization—a career destination for top talent among managers as well as staff— is fundamental to ensuring ongoing product and service development, customer satisfaction, and financial success.

Tying It All Together

We have already discussed the value of formal and informal mentors to help employees and managers at all levels not only with situational (tactical) needs, but also with skills development (strategic) needs. To speed your own development of essential skills, get a mentor. If you already have a mentor, get a second one to gain an additional perspective. Mentors can help you to achieve better metric scores. (For additional ways to approach skill development for your employees and for yourself, see chapter 8, "Skill Builder.")

Your individual performance as a people manager matters. It is the backbone of your personal brand in the organization. Your mastery of the metrics that matter will make your day-to-day job experience less stressful because staff turnover will be lower while production and quality levels will be higher. Senior management will notice. Your individual performance determines your marketability inside and outside your organization. You should track the wins: the employees you promote (including those to another department), your assimilation of new hires so they reach their full productivity faster, and so on. Your attention to people management means that your employees will be engaged and committed to the success of not just themselves, but also to the success of their peers, their department, their organization, and their manager—you!

Blue Money and Green Money Turnover Cost Calculations

NOTICE PERIOD

Green Money (actual) Costs:

1. Last paycheck, accrued vacation, separation pay $ _____
2. Increased unemployment tax $ _____
3. Continued benefits $ _____

Blue Money Costs
(appropriate salary/hour × time spent on each activity):

1. Administrative costs for processing the separation: $ _____
   process benefits; contact unemployment office,
   Payroll, IS departments; schedule exit interview; etc.
2. Lower productivity: employee, peers, supervisor, subordinates $ _____
3. Exit interview, transition meetings $ _____

VACANCY PERIOD

Green Money (actual) Costs:

1. Advertising and recruiter fees $ _____
2. Interview expenses (meals, mileage, or other) $ _____
3. Printing costs for company marketing materials $ _____
4. Assessments $ _____
5. Criminal checks, reference checks, credit checks, etc. $ _____
6. Medical exams and drug tests $ _____
7. Temporary/contract employee costs $ _____
8. Overtime costs $ _____
9. Relocation expenses and salary $ _____

Blue Money Costs
(appropriate salary/hour × time spent on each activity):

1. Lost productivity: peers, supervisor, subordinates $ _____
2. Advertising creation and placement $ _____
3. Recruiter selection $ _____
4. Administrative costs: ordering forms and copies of annual reports, $ _____
   scheduling and scoring assessments, coordinating with hiring $ _____
   manager and others, etc. $ _____
5. Resume screening $ _____
6. Interviews: first, second, third $ _____

HIRING/ORIENTATION PERIOD

Green Money (actual) Costs:

1. Orientation materials (handbook, video, handouts, etc.) $ _____
2. Formal training programs (materials, course fees) $ _____
3. Informal one-on-one training (materials, if any) $ _____

Blue Money Costs
(appropriate salary/hour × time spent on each activity):

1. Orientation participants' salaries $ _____
2. Lost productivity: peers, supervisor, subordinates $ _____
3. Administrative costs: orientation setup, ordering $ _____
   materials, etc.
4. Informal training and one-on-ones $ _____

HIDDEN COSTS

1. Missed deadlines and shipments $ _____
2. Loss of organization knowledge $ _____
3. Lower morale due to overwork $ _____
4. Learning curve $ _____
5. Client issues due to turnover $ _____
6. Loss of client relationships $ _____
7. Disrupted department operations $ _____
8. Chain reaction turnover $ _____

TOTAL REPLACEMENT COST $ _____

Source: Nancy S. Ahlrichs, *Competing for Talent: Key Recruitment and Retention Strategies for Becoming an Employer of Choice* (Palo Alto, CA: Davies-Black Publishing, 2001), 14–15. Reprinted with permission.

Discussion Questions

1. If experiences are the critical source of value for your employees (consumers of the work experience), how would they describe their experience of you? Would on-site staff use the same descriptors as off-site staff? What desirable descriptors might on-site or off-site employees omit altogether in describing you?

2. What professional organizations might you join to create an external peer group? What community groups might provide another external peer group? How could you tap into these peer groups to uncover the manager performance metrics being used successfully in other organizations?

3. Ask your formal or informal mentor to review the three types of people management metrics listed in this chapter and to write down three from each category on a piece of paper. You repeat the same exercise. Compare your lists and discuss why each of you made your specific selections.

4. Use your combined and refined list of metrics that matter as the basis of a preliminary discussion with your manager and/or with Human Resources personnel. Get their agreement to design an updated performance management process that better reflects the metrics that matter in your area.

Resources

To learn more about performance management—yours and that of your staff—read:

Creating Commitment by Michael N. O'Malley. New York: John Wiley and Sons, 2000.

Effective Phrases for Performance Appraisals by James E. Neal, Jr. Perrysburg, OH: Neal Publications, 2000.

Motivation Management by Thad Green. Palo Alto, CA: Davies-Black Publishing, 2000.

A Stake in the Outcome by Jack Stack and Bo Burlingham. New York: Doubleday, 2002.

To gather employees' input on their experience of management practices, work with your Human Resources partner and speed your online search via a "library of assessments" such as that found at the Performance Assessment Network or www.pantesting.com. Check out assessment tools such as the following:

AskEmployees.com, an Internet-based survey tool that provides real-time feedback that helps companies understand what is really important to their employees. See www.walkerinfo.com.

Checkpoint 360, one of several Internet-based assessment tools provided by Profiles International to guide management development. See www. profilesinternational.com.

Employee Relationship Report, an innovative study that measures employee commitment levels and work factors, giving management objective information to identify and address problematic areas. See www.walker info.com.

The Human Resource Climate Survey (HRCS I), a 90-item survey that has been administered to over 200,000 participants nationwide. See www.bauerandassociates.com.

The Leadership Assessment Survey (LAS), a 360-degree feedback instrument that measures an individual's leadership in sixteen competency sets. See www.cci4360.com.

Management-Leadership Practices Inventory (MLPI), a norm-based, 360-degree feedback instrument that assesses a supervisor's management and leadership skills. See www.pantesting.com.

Performance Feedback & Coaching, a 360-degree Web-based employee performance and improvement system that provides a means of giving and receiving feedback from multiple perspectives. See www.walkerinfo.com.

The SimpleSurvey.com, an award-winning Web-based survey system that allows companies the flexibility to customize and distribute surveys on their own stakeholders. See www.walkerinfo.com.

Part Two

Developing the Five Competencies of Managers of Choice

Talent Scouter

"56 percent of employees have made plans to leave,
are actively looking or are open to a move."

**—"The Towers Perrin Talent Report 2001:
New Realities in Today's Workforce"**[1]

With so many available potential hires, you must be hearing from
dozens of qualified candidates. Raise your hand if you are satisfied
with delegating all recruiting and hiring to the Human Resources
department or to outsourced agencies and recruiters. You may also
raise your hand if you are a manager in Human Resources or one of
the outsourced agencies or recruiting firms and you are satisfied
with the current arrangement. If you are a recent hire, raise your
hand if the hiring process excited you even more about working for
the company than before you applied. If you are one of the lucky
managers who is working well with HR to bring in more high-
quality candidates than you can possibly handle, great! If not, let's

turn you into a talent scouter, and your organization and your department into talent magnets.

Top talent is fundamental to the performance of your department and your organization. It is also fundamental to keeping your stress level low. You cannot afford to passively outsource every aspect of the selection and hiring process to your HR department. Since one technically qualified candidate does not "equal" another, neither you nor HR will be satisfied with the results. A "great hire" has more than certifications, degrees, or even experience.

You and HR must commit to working together to solve immediate as well as predictable hiring needs. This requires attracting a diverse array of talent, creating a pipeline of qualified talent for future hiring needs, and providing a "wow!" experience to applicants and candidates. This also means virtually blowing up the current hiring process and starting over—using different strategies and tactics—and partnering with HR. Hiring presents the perfect opportunity for quality and efficiency to intersect with innovation and creativity.

The good news about the 56 percent of employees in the Towers Perrin report who plan to leave their jobs, and the 50.5 percent of Conference Board survey respondents who state that they are not satisfied with their current position,[2] is that you have the opportunity to hire top talent for nearly every position on your roster. If you think that only the youngest employees are restless, think again. The bad news is that less half of the 35–44 age group (down from 60 percent) and the 55–64 age group are satisfied. On one hand, this means that you will be able to hire people at virtually every career level, but it also means that you will need to fend off other employers who want to hire your existing employees. The key will be to re-recruit top talent of all ages in your department and manage them better than anyone ever managed you.

In this chapter we explore your role as talent scouter in bringing diverse top talent to the table. The balance of part 2 is focused on developing the competencies that will enable you to grow and retain the top talent you hire.

Partnering with HR to Improve Hiring Results

For too long, hiring managers have been at odds with the recruiters in the Human Resources department about the speed of hiring and quality of candidates needed. Managers with one or more job openings are swamped trying to pacify overloaded employees who are struggling to meet production or project goals in spite of holes in their teams. HR has federal and state compliance requirements, extremely small recruiting budgets, and unending numbers of requisitions to juggle. Typically, managers pressure HR to "get 'em in here *now*," while HR has to ensure that candidates meet minimum qualifications and skill requirements, pass background and drug checks, and will agree to pay packages that fit the organization's overall compensation philosophy.

Hiring quality candidates quickly is critical, but most organizations have not made recruiting a true priority. Overworked managers just want good candidates from which to choose but are unaware that their role is so critical. An "ideal candidate" may be turned off by the hiring manager's lukewarm interview style or lost altogether before an interview can take place because the swamped hiring manager has no time to interview before the top talent has been hired by a competitor. The prize of top talent goes to the manager whose interview skills are as sharp as his or her other technical skills (see "What's Working" on page 110), and to the HR recruiting manager who ensures that the candidate's total job-shopping experience stands out from that of other talent competitors. If any part of the hiring experience is a turn-off, candidates will seek another employer. Yesterday's approach does not catch the imagination of today's consumer of the work experience.

Outcompete Your Talent Competitors

Top talent is being hired elsewhere because your talent competitors have a stronger employee value proposition or employment brand. Every experience a candidate has with your organization—with the advertising, on your website, your response time, lag time between

What's Working at The Container Store

Practice makes perfect, especially when it comes to developing interview skills. New managers at The Container Store—selected by the Great Place to Work® Institute as one of the "100 Best Companies to Work For"—learn to master interviewing by role-playing and later conducting live interviews while more experienced managers sit in.[3] Mentoring from these "master interviewers," as well as observation and repeated practice, builds new manager confidence, interview skills, and hiring success rates. At The Container Store, no one underestimates the power of a great interview experience.

interview and follow-up, the receptionist's greeting, chance "hellos" to talented potential peers, and your preparation for the interview—validates or refutes your organization's reputation as a terrific place to work. Candidate, not just employee, experiences make up your organization's employment brand. Candidates use instant messaging to quickly tell fifty to one hundred others about their interview experience—and they name names. Together with your HR partner, you can enhance those experiences and rocket your hiring practices into the twenty-first century by updating the following:

Job descriptions. Your organization needs updated job descriptions that include the competencies (combined skills and behaviors) of star performers. Including competencies automatically eliminates average performers from the initial selection process and should be integrated into the interview and reference-checking processes.

Application media and processes. Your talent competitors make it easy for top talent to use a range of methods to apply—online, on paper, in person, and so on—and they use software not only to respond quickly to questions but also to notify applicants if they are selected to interview. The software can also inform even casual applicants when an appropriate job becomes available. Does your organization's website show photos of real employees and typical relationship-building and community activities? What about organizational awards, employee community involvement, or client information? Is it possible to take initial skills assessments online? Can the applicant ask questions and get them answered in a timely manner?

If HR is in the process of evaluating software products to automate portions of the recruiting process, you could volunteer to be on the software selection task force or to pilot a new process or product. Invite several recent hires as well as one or two recent "declines" to participate.

Interview skills. Ask HR to locate and conduct an interactive interview skills training program for all hiring managers. Adults learn by doing—not by reading, thinking, or talking about a new skill. How well you interview candidates not only determines the quality of the ultimate hires, but also strongly influences candidates' decision to join your team. In today's hiring marketplace, you need special pointers for interviewing diverse candidates. To feel comfortable with more than one type of interview, and with a variety of diverse candidates, practice your interview skills with another manager.

Interview questions. Team with HR to develop a standard set of questions for each position in your department, starting with the position that has the most turnover or is expected to have the most growth. Ensure that the questions uncover the candidate's values and enable the candidate to tell stories that demonstrate he or she has the competencies to be a star. Do not rest until you have developed questions for each position that reports to you. File them for later use. After six months or more, however, check with HR to ensure a match with current job descriptions and that the questions continue to be in compliance with the latest legal requirements.

Toward the end of the interview process, consider adding three questions that may separate otherwise similar candidates:

- "If I met your current/past manager at a social event, what would he or she tell me about you?"

- "How would you fill in this sentence? 'Every day, I come in to work prepared to _____.'"

- "Please tell me what three things will determine whether you accept an offer from us?"

Skill verification processes. Team with HR to develop or select real-world tests to augment interview responses. For promising candidates, request that they demonstrate relevant skills to the job using the following:

- **Skill tests.** These can be purchased or developed and might include math, writing, computer, engineering, or other skills. Select skills appropriate to the position.

- **Role-playing.** If appropriate, ask the candidate to role-play scenarios with a difficult customer, a first-time prospect, and so on. Another variation is an in-box exercise. Today's timed role-plays utilize paper and online elements.

- **Action plans.** Ask candidates to outline a marketing or sales plan, or even a plan for their first thirty days on the job.

- **Creative projects.** For candidates who must have strong writing or building skills, give an actual assignment with a realistic deadline.

- **Presentations.** Ask top sales or trainer candidates to prepare a brief presentation for the next interview.

Personality assessments. In the final phases of interviewing, work with your HR department to select a personality assessment to help determine a good fit between the candidate and your culture. Assessments are intended to augment the interview process by providing information that is otherwise difficult to uncover. While it is fairly easy to verify a candidate's hard skills, many employers want more information about personality fit such as truthfulness or speed of decision making.

Literally thousands of personality assessments are available, so you must be careful and diligent in trying to find just the right one to help you predict behavior and performance. A reliable assessment provides scores that do not change over time. It also measures what it was designed to measure. Inappropriate assessments may measure irrelevant competencies or psychological parameters, discriminate against racial or ethnic groups, or violate candidates' rights to privacy. To determine an assessment's reliability and validity, ask to see the list of research studies performed on the assessment (a minimum of 15–20 studies by recognized professionals is desirable). Here are some additional guidelines:

- **Normal range measurements.** When evaluating a generic personality assessment, make sure that the assessment is designed to measure normal personality; tools used to measure abnormal personality may put your organization at risk from a legal standpoint. The most commonly recognized factors in normal personality are emotional stability/instability, extroversion/introversion, agreeability/contentiousness, and being open/closed to experiences. While different language might be used to label these factors, most industrial psychologists have reached agreement on their use.

- **Success predictors.** Many service providers sell generic assessments to predict a candidate's ability to achieve success in occupations such as sales, management, customer service, etc. Other providers will help your organization to develop a customized profile as a predictor of success in a specific position. If you choose to develop a customized profile for specific positions, select an experienced consultant to assist with the process and insist that he or she monitor its effectiveness.

- **Role of environment or culture.** Each person's behavior is influenced by personality as well as environment (or organizational culture), so the personal characteristics of the top performer in one organization are likely to differ from those of the top performer in another organization. Generic assessments may be best suited for use in organizations that do not have distinctive cultures. For example, a successful product sales representative in an organization with a numbers-oriented sales strategy (e.g., X sales calls per day) may have a difficult time in an organization that focuses on relationship development, repeat sales, and long-term client relationships. The personality characteristics needed to succeed in one situation may not match those needed in another.

- **Overreliance on assessment results.** Assessments that do not measure appropriate characteristics can needlessly screen out potentially successful employees. Use common sense even with well-known personality profiles when evaluating candidates. The use of the appropriate assessment for each position is critical to minimizing the chance of legal recourse from those candidates not hired.

Background checks. Due to the increasing number of big settlements in court cases as well as the attacks of September 11, no employer can afford to neglect background verification processes. Employers can validate relevant items such as criminal record, social security number, employment history, education, driving record, credit history, worker's compensation claims, and civil court records. These checks may take as little as one to three days, but be patient—employers can be held liable and/or receive bad publicity for hiring frauds, illegal aliens, violent offenders, or other inappropriate employees. Falsehoods on resumes are, of course, common. In 2001, for example, 25 percent of background checks conducted by A Matter of Fact, a Sacramento, California, firm, uncovered issues with job titles, dates of employment, and salary; 44 percent of 2.6 million background checks conducted by ADP Screening and Selection Services showed discrepancies in credentials, licenses, and education.[4]

Cultural introduction. The interview process is a mutual sales exercise. The candidate has his or her skills, energy, and aspirations to sell to the organization, and you have the open position, training and development, environment, opportunity to work with talented peers, and potential career movement to sell to the candidate. The tighter the hiring market, the more the employer is in a sales role. Remember, everything that happens from the moment the candidate steps foot on your property sends a message about the employment brand and culture:

- Is security tight—but courteous and speedy?

- Is the reception area dimly lit and decorated with plastic plants and worn furniture, and is the candidate left to make a phone call to connect to the desired department? Or is the candidate welcomed by the receptionist and made to feel comfortable?

- Are several other candidates filling out the same application on a clipboard?

- Is the candidate introduced as "the 11 o'clock candidate" or by name?

- Is the hiring manager late, unprepared, and impatient to move on to the next meeting? Or is the hiring manager on time, prepared for the interview, and at ease?

The importance of people in the culture comes through loud and clear in the spoken and unspoken messages sent to the candidate.

As a hiring manager, you must take an active role in the recruiting process. Partner with HR to accomplish your mutual goals—it can be the start of an even broader relationship that will accelerate your understanding of the organization and the broader world of management. Your confidence with interviewing and better knowledge of the overall process will enable HR to do a better job of screening for the top talent needed in your department.

Every candidate is a unique mix of personality, interests, talents, and experiences. Learn to think like a job seeker/consumer! Call in to get more information and see what happens. Park where candidates park and walk into the building where they walk in. What do you see? Does the receptionist greet you? This is a good start, but first you have to locate the right candidates.

Talent Scouting 101: Identifying Top Talent

Most of us believe that we will "know it when we see it" for a lot of things, including top talent. This method guarantees that we will *not* get the candidates we want because top talent's competencies vary widely from one position to another. Avoid relying on your gut feelings because your stress level or mood during the interview may influence your gut. It pays to be specific about star competencies in the open positions in your department. If you don't have an updated job description and a success profile to compare candidates against, you may be tempted to hire someone for their hard skills or years of experience and not for their fit with the job or the culture. The only way to duplicate past hiring successes is to zero in on the specific aspects of successful stars. See "What's Working" on page 117.

Star performers stand out by going beyond the listed qualifications and job description. They receive above-average ratings—not just from you, but from others including clients and peers. What are the characteristics of a star performer in your organization? What it takes to be a standout as an on-site, entry-level accounts payable representative is likely to be very different from what it takes for an entry-level trainer with a three-state region to cover. The basic positions differ as do required behaviors. The accounts payable

What's Working at Emmis Communications

"A successful radio account executive is a quick, customer-oriented problem solver who can juggle a million things at once, follow through on the details, yet be flexible when the client wants changes. And they have to be fun people," says Mary Young, sales manager for Indianapolis-based WYXB and WENS-FM, two of twenty-three radio stations owned by Emmis Communications. "Experience doesn't always foreshadow success, so we use an assessment based on a specific profile—and I keep my eyes open for the tenacious, passionate candidates no matter their work experience."

One of her most successful hires has been JoLynn Shallop, an ex-paralegal and ex-jewelry store marketing assistant. "I mailed my resume and then walked my resume over to the director of Sales. I kept calling and following up because I wanted an interview," says Shallop. "I believe in radio advertising as a valid way to build our customer's businesses, and I specifically wanted to work in the Emmis culture because their reps love their jobs. They get great training and are routinely asked to brainstorm ways to make the company a better place to work."

Emmis sales managers are willing to hire for competencies and then train in product and sales skills. "If I looked only at her resume, it would not have predicted success. First, I noticed JoLynn's tenacity and then her assessment scores. This is a difficult job, where the reps get five 'nos' for every 'yes,'" adds Young. "Successful account executives enjoy the full range of activities from cold-calling to creating commercial copy to collecting payments. We have fun, but we all work long hours. The assessments help to uncover the candidates with career motivation as well as the competencies to handle the full sales cycle. You can't hire the people you need if you don't know what you are looking for."

representative might need to have terrific analytical, written, and oral communication (telephone) skills as well as follow-through. The entry-level trainer might need to possess excellent presentation skills as well as written skills to be persuasive, to empower others, and so on. Ideally, both would demonstrate initiative and be results oriented.

Five Steps to Develop Star Competencies

Too often we hire for hard skills and fire for lack of soft skills. We focus on hard skills in the job description, interview, and reference-checking processes as well as in training on the job—and are surprised when the employee does not display the soft skills we assumed he or she possessed. Employees at any level are almost never terminated for lack of hard skills. Ask Human Resources for help in clarifying the complete list of behavioral competencies—or soft skills—for jobs in your department. To improve hiring outcomes, you can take the following steps:

- Partnering with HR, ask incumbents in the selected position to review the current job description and return it to you with any additions or corrections.

- In a small group setting, with your HR representative as the facilitator, analyze the position for five to seven behaviors (competencies) necessary to the success of the position. How do these competencies fit the organization's values? Gain consensus from the incumbents on final changes to the overall responsibilities of the job.

- If any of the current incumbents are star performers, interview them separately and record their behavioral statements to uncover the additional competencies that garner the "star" rating. As manager, do you agree with these assessments? Do these additional competencies fit the organization's values?

- Since past behavior predicts future behavior, develop an up-dated job description that includes the competencies of your star performers. Develop interview questions that allow candi-dates to give examples of their using the needed competencies.

- As an additional step, build development plans for all incum-bents to enhance their use of star competencies.

Develop Competency-Based Interview Questions

To ensure that you consistently hire top talent, develop a specific list of interview questions that are used for all candidates for each posi-tion in your department. The key is to avoid asking, "What would you do if . . ." because those answers come from the imagination of the candidate. We can all imagine ourselves being successful. Instead, draw out the candidate's actual behaviors in specific situa-tions. Make yourself a grid of competencies and questions like the one shown in table 6.

Once you have developed the competency-based interview questions, meet with your HR partner to review the question list and to determine which questions are best suited for initial inter-views and which are best asked during second or subsequent inter-views. Practice using the questions by mock-interviewing your mentor, a peer from your MOC community, or your HR partner. Remember, in the long run it is easier and faster to hire for compe-tencies and train for hard skills.

Create a Pipeline of Diverse Top Talent

Factors in diversity have traditionally included gender, race, national origin, religion, ethnicity, and age. Many organizations are expanding the definition to include sexual orientation and even thinking styles. Very soon, diversity will include the wide variety of working relationships—full-time and part-time workers,

Table 6 Competency Question Template		
Competency/ Descriptor	**Specific Question**	**Structure the Answer**
Initiative Identifies what needs to be done and takes action before being asked.	What would be an example of a time when you spotted something that needed to be done and took care of it before being asked?	For each competency question, ask the candidate to share his or her experience by telling you: What was the situation? What did you do? What was the result? How did you feel about it?
Seeks out others involved in the situation to learn perspectives.	In what situation at work have you sought out others to get their views before taking action yourself?	
Takes action to change the direction of events.	Have you ever realized that something was not going well and decided to take action to correct it?	
Stress Management Handles multiple problems or tasks at once.	When have you had three to five competing "priorities"? How did you handle the pressure of the moment?	
Maintains a sense of humor under difficult circumstances.	When have you used humor to defuse a difficult situation?	
Controls his or her response when criticized, provoked, or attacked.	Can you describe a situation where you handled a dissatisfied customer or peer?	

teleworkers, project staff, and so on. The younger your workforce, the more diverse it will be.

Maintaining a diverse workforce—and spreading the word about it—is good business. Research has shown that companies that do the best job of communicating the diversity of their workforce are often the companies with the highest revenue share in their industry.[5] According to 91 percent of survey respondents from Fortune 1000 companies and the list of "100 Best Companies to Work For,"[6] diversity helps organizations to keep a competitive advantage.

Your organization must become a "diversity magnet" and a center for innovation to be able to attract and retain all types of diverse top talent. To do that, you and your organization must go beyond "know-how" to "know-who."[7] To diversify and expand your range of potential candidates, network inside and outside your department and organization; uncover well-connected individuals with diverse contacts, professional and civic organizations with diverse members, and schools with a diverse student body. Your internal and external network will enable you to acquire, transform, and apply that know-how so that innovation can occur. We each have our own circle of family, friends, colleagues, school chums, and so on that make up a "know-who" network. Know-who cannot be delegated, but it can be amplified through the networks of others.

As the personification of your organization's culture, you can build a brand as a diversity magnet by doing more than posting your organization's nondiscrimination policy and waiting for great candidates to appear. Consider adopting the following "best practices" as defined by Barbara Frankel in "The Top 10 Companies for Diversity Recruitment and Retention":[8]

- Ensure participation of all employees in your organization's mentoring programs (Verizon Communications)

- Develop and use metrics to assess your diversity recruiting, promotion, and retention successes (Deloitte & Touche, Pitney Bowes, Verizon Communications)

- Encourage your employees to celebrate and communicate their diversity

- In collaboration with HR, initiate or expand affinity groups for Asians, African Americans, Latinos, gays and lesbians, employees with disabilities, and women (Procter & Gamble)

- Encourage the expansion and use of domestic partner benefits (Sempra Energy)

- Join and encourage employees to join and become active in multicultural organizations (American Airlines, JP Morgan Chase)

- In collaboration with HR, develop performance and behavioral competencies for managing, leveraging, and leading diverse employees to create a culture of inclusion (Eastman Kodak)

- Develop and distribute to all employees a diversity scorecard that includes demographics of the organization as a whole, attendance at diversity events, participation in mentoring and networking activities, training and development figures, supplier diversity rates, employee satisfaction rates, amount of business conducted with diverse markets, if appropriate, etc. (JP Morgan Chase)

- Invite employees to become involved in philanthropic support for diverse communities (IBM)

- Set goals for employee participation in work–life balance programs; top talent wants work configuration choices (IBM, Prudential Financial)

- Display your organization's diversity commitment prominently on your website, including (with permission) photos of real employees

- Encourage outreach to multicultural students (Prudential Financial)

- Provide mentors to all college interns

- Teach part-time or as a guest lecturer at local community colleges and universities to create relationships with diverse candidates and referral sources

Become knowledgeable about your organization's racial and other demographic information so that you can answer job candidates' questions about the makeup of your organization's board of directors, senior executives, vice presidents, and middle managers. Be ready to discuss your organization's diversity efforts including mentoring programs, affinity groups, development courses, sponsored events, and so on. Many candidates will want to know what your organization is doing in this area.

Tap Nontraditional Sources for Top Talent

If you want a diverse range of top talent who will ignite your department's innovation initiatives, you may need to forget everything you think you know about attracting candidates. For starters, with HR check your organization's website for diversity attractors, as described in "Five Tips for an Effective Website" on page 124 Nearly every candidate or casual job seeker will check your organization's website before proceeding with an initial contact. What information could a candidate glean from the website and job description? Are FAQs available? Is there another way for candidates to get their questions answered? Try to apply for a position using your organization's website.

The next step is to find appropriate candidates. Know-who trumps know-how in the search for top talent. Diverse top talent can be located 24/7/365 if you know where to look or how to get their attention. Consider the following possibilities:

- **Internal candidates.** Give priority to qualified internal candidates or those who could grow quickly into the job. Be a cheerleader for career development. It is easier to train for any hard

Five Tips for an Effective Website

Sixteen percent of an organization's total hires come through its website.[9] Every other candidate resource—even Internet job boards—is going to funnel candidates to your website, so it had better grab your attention immediately! In addition to showcasing your organization's services and clients, vision and values, organizational or departmental awards, recent press releases, and current job opportunities, an effective website will

- Feature a "Getting to Know Us" video clip, or a "virtual" tour of the organization and a "Day in the Life" video clip for as many positions as possible

- Encourage online job applications that do not require laborious rekeying of entire resumes

- Enable online assessments for required technical skills

- Prominently display benefits such as childcare/eldercare support, flextime options, etc.

- Enable a casual job seeker to ask questions and be informed when an appropriate position opens

skills that are needed. If you have one or more openings for which you would normally administer a pre-employment assessment (e.g., an IT opening or other job typically requiring an online assessment to measure cognitive ability, vocational and mathematical skills, verbal reasoning, or other competencies), ask current employees to take the assessment. You may uncover a hidden wealth of talent among your organization's clerks, typists, and administrators or others who would appreciate the career opportunity and who could quickly be trained for the technical skills necessary for the job.[10]

- **Employee and alumni referrals.** Your current and past employees know the culture and what it takes to succeed in your organization. Provide rewards and recognition for these unofficial recruiters. Pay promptly, publicly, and completely—don't deduct taxes from the reward.

- **Professional organizations.** Join and get active in local, state, and national professional organizations and watch your candidate pipeline fill. Join online discussion groups and message boards. Connect directly with potential candidates rather than reviewing potentially outdated resumes. Post your openings including star competencies and receive star responses!

- **Past "declines," "#2s," and applicants rejected due to hiring freezes.** Qualified "near misses" too often are lost in the heat of daily business. Create a file for later contacts. If it broke your heart to be declined, disappoint a "close #2," or have to tell a top talent candidate about your hiring freeze, go to your files and recontact him or her today! Send e-mails and handwritten notes to candidates you hope to hire when your budget grows. Invite the "best of the best" to breakfast or lunch just to stay in touch. If you have the resources, pay the perfect candidates to wait or slot them into current openings temporarily.

- **Affinity groups.** Encourage affinity groups to recruit qualified candidates for posted openings.

- **Disabled individuals.** A thirty-year study by DuPont found that job performance by employees with disabilities was equal or better than their fully functioning peers, with safety, attendance, and loyalty records far above the norm. Washington Mutual's call center turnover among employees with disabilities is 10–15 percent while overall turnover is 40 percent. These studies bode well for the employment prospects of qualified candidates with disabilities.[11] According to the U.S. Census Bureau, in 2000, 30.6 milllion people in the U.S., or 19.2 percent, between ages

21 and 64 had a disability; of that population, 56.6 percent were employed. Log on to find qualified candidates through www.pcepd.gov, www.abletowork.org, www.jobaccess.org, www.justonebreak.com, www.hirepotential.org, or www.ssa.gov/work.

- **Experienced temps for seasonal work.** Hire semi-retired former corporate executives and other experienced individuals for seasonal positions. You will pay a bit more—and get a lot more!

- **Eastern European, Asian, and African students for seasonal work.** English-speaking students from foreign countries can significantly offset your need for summer hires. Consider subsidized housing plus end-of-summer bonuses of $1 per hour or more if the 10- to 12-week work agreement is fulfilled.

- **Minority suppliers.** These suppliers know your culture and can make excellent recommendations if they know details about your openings.

- **Associations.** To find appropriate professionals, go to the appropriate professional association. For sources, check http://info.asaenet.org/Gateway/OnlineAssocSlist.html.

- **Television ads.** Local cable channels including USA, WTBS, TNT, "E," Comedy Central, MTV, and so on reach candidates who are not looking. The typical cost is $500 for production and less than $10 per spot.

- **Radio ads and job fairs.** Ask current employees, including late-shift employees, to name their favorite radio stations. Be where your candidates are, when your candidates are available.

- **Job-share teams.** Consider promoting current job-share teams in your organization.

- **High school and college alumni connections.** Build relationships between your organization and target schools through your employees.

- **Trainable rookies and older workers.** For IT and other fast-changing functions, hire rookies straight out of college or older workers with a burning desire to learn. Use training and flex-time as magnets. Offer fun, creativity, and the opportunity to work with younger employees—not just to attract Gen Y applicants, but also to attract older employees.[12]

Tying It All Together

While overall knowledge increases over time, a team can become less open to new methods or ideas, more complacent, and predictable to the competition. Teams actually become less productive the longer they are together due to "knowledge ossification,"[13] so it is important to welcome new talent to the team.

You are not alone in your quest for top talent. Because you have talent-seeking competition, it is important to continue your recruiting activities after the offer has been accepted. Consult your other employees to develop an effective process for staying in touch before day one and creating a calendar of welcoming events and processes that send the message, "We are glad you are here. Join us and make a difference!"

By aligning your recruitment efforts with your organization's business plan, recruiting employees who are well-equipped to perform their duties, and actively engendering trust and a relationship with new hires, you can become a premier talent scouter who gets fast, qualified results and maintains a continuous pipeline of talent.[14] Use and expand your know-who and reward your employees for doing the same. Personalize and speed up your response to all candidates, particularly Gen Y candidates, to increase the odds of snagging the top talent you desire. A quick response is seen as a sign of respect—and it is seen rarely enough to make you stand out.

Discussion Questions

1. Do you have an HR partner? If not, determine who your logical HR partner would be and set up a lunch meeting away from the office ASAP. Brainstorm ways you can help each other in the competition for top talent.

2. Have you developed competencies for at least one position that reports to you? Have you developed competencies for all the positions that report to you? Make this a topic at your meeting with your HR partner.

3. It helps to put yourself in the shoes of a candidate to streamline the process and increase your odds of hiring top talent. What happens when you apply for a position with your organization from an outside computer? What happens when you apply for a position from inside your organization? As the candidate, do you know what to expect and are you promptly contacted? If not, ask to be on a cross-functional task force to improve the process.

4. Too often we do not get a second chance to make a better first impression. Ask individuals hired in the last year—and those who dropped out along the way—to provide their insights about your interview skills, the organization's process, and how to improve the hiring experience at your organization.

5. Do you have interview questions that cover the competencies for each of the positions in your department? Have you practiced the questions—as well as salary negotiation—with your HR partner or mentor? If not, call for a meeting today! Be ready for your next hire!

6. How many potential candidates do you have in your files if your best employee leaves? Consult your current employees to develop your mutual know-who skills through attending together and/or sponsoring an upcoming professional organization meeting or other activity designed to meet future diverse top talent for your department.

Resources

To learn more about competencies and how to use them to develop better job descriptions, performance management criteria, and development plans, read:

The Value Added Employee by Edward J. Cripe and Richard S. Mansfield. Burlington, MA: Butterworth-Heinermann, 2002.

For software to determine competencies, contact www.ddiworld.com for information about Identifying Criteria for Success (ICS).

To learn more about finding qualified diverse top talent, read:

America's Workforce Is Coming of Age by Catherine D. Fyock, A.E.P. New York: Lexington Books, 1990.

Competing for Talent by Nancy S. Ahlrichs. Palo Alto, CA: Davies-Black Publishing, 2000.

Finding Diversity by Luby Ismail and Alexander Kronemer. Alexandria, VA: Society for Human Resource Management, 2002.

Get the Best by Catherine D. Fyock. Crestwood, KY: Innovative Management Concepts, 1993.

Winning the Talent Wars by Bruce Tulgan. New York: W. W. Norton and Company, 2001.

To learn more about formulating great interview questions, read:

Hiring Top Performers: 350 Great Interview Questions for People Who Need People by Carol A. Hacker. Alpharetta, GA: Carol A. Hacker Associates, 2002.

Relationship Builder

"Synergy is to teams what energy is to the individual."

—**Karp, Fuller, and Sirias,** *Bridging the Boomer-Xer Gap*[1]

Great people managers manage individuals individually. Managers become managers of choice (MOCs) when they capture their employees' "heartshare," not just "mindshare." They inspire passion in their people, no matter what the job at hand. It is passion, or heartshare, that motivates employees beyond merely doing their job. To encourage commitment and engage employees' heartshare, MOCs must be great relationship builders.

For a variety of reasons, the offer of money and titles no longer inspires passion in three out of four generations, especially when these offers are in place of other motivators. (It is understandable how Gen Y employees might be passionate about earning more than entry-level wages.) Research by the American Productivity and Quality Center shows that it takes a 5–8 percent increase in wages to change behavior,[2] while other research puts the figure at 15 percent or more. At early career stages, higher-percentage raises are more common. But for most of us, raises have stagnated at 4 percent or less for the past decade, and in our smaller or less hierarchical organizations there simply are not enough promotions to go around. Raises and promotions, even when available, do not inspire passion in Veterans who have hit the ceiling of pay and titles and are looking for ways to wind down their career. They also don't appeal to Baby Boomers who are opting for increased work–life balance or to Gen Xers who decline any promotion that takes them away from their young family.

Few employees finding themselves in a negative relationship with their manager or their peers (except perhaps mercenaries and those trapped without choices) will stay long in their position, no matter their compensation or title. For your on-site and off-site employees, a positive relationship with you is fundamental to a positive work experience. At a time of so many career choices, with reasonably competitive pay, employees will choose to work for managers who provide respect, opportunities for learning and achievement, and an enjoyable work experience that will accommodate a private life.

Relationship building is the foundation competency of great people managers. At a time when passion is needed to fuel innovation and creativity, MOCs know they must manage each employee differently in order to understand each one's motivators. MOCs know that every day is an opportunity to develop the level of professional relationship with employees—some of whom will enable the department as a whole to step up to new technology, adjust to a new organizational design, or overcome tough competition by translating customer needs into new services and products.

In this chapter we discuss how MOCs build relationships with new hires even before day one; encourage relationship building among employees, with other departments, and with the external community; coach employees to maximize performance; and use technology to enhance relationships.

The Hierarchy of Relationship

Business success happens "people to people to people"[3]—requiring know-who in addition to know-how. In a work environment, an employee has four types of relationships:

- A relationship with the manager (you)

- Multiple relationships with peers

- Relationships with one or more other departments

- Multiple relationships with the community (customers, vendors, client and candidate referral sources, civic and professional organizations, feeder schools, neighborhoods, city governments, etc.)

As a quick exercise, list all your employees. For each one, assign a score of 1 (poor or low) to 25 (excellent or high) for each of the four types of relationships listed above. Add each employee's points to get individual scores—100 is not expected. Next, do the same for yourself. Where are your group's relationship strengths? With each other? Between your department and other relevant departments? Where are *your* strengths?

If you are to lead a group that becomes known for innovation and creativity, you need to foster excellence in all four types of relationships. For some individuals, relationship building is easy, but positive relationships take conscious effort on the part of everyone. Relationships are two-way; so are the benefits. The effort is worthwhile because the quality of your relationships determines the quality of your work experiences and output and, ultimately, your value to the organization. This is the case for all employees, no matter their level. Remember that excellent relationship builders tend to rise in organizations, while poor relationship builders are shunted to backwater assignments or out the door.

In the words of Ken Martlage, organizational performance consultant and president of Phoenix Images, "Success and productivity—getting the work done—are the desired end results that

Figure 2 Hierarchy of Relationship

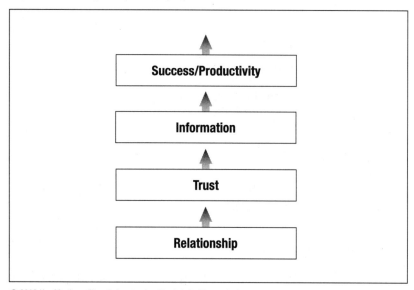

© 2002 Ken Martlage, Phoenix Images, Inc. Reprinted with permission.

cannot occur without the ready flow of information that flows freely along lines of trust between individuals." Ongoing creativity and innovation cannot exist in a work environment that lacks positive relationships. Two people working together require more than a superficial relationship if more than minimum performance is expected. According to Martlage, "By interacting, communicating, and spending time together . . . focusing on building relationships, we can genuinely increase trust, which in turn develops improved channels of communication and information flow, and results in greater potential for success and productivity."[4] That formula is made graphic in figure 2.

In *The 8 Practices of Exceptional Companies,* Jac Fitz-enz lists communication, partnering with stakeholders (across functions inside as well as outside the organization), and collaboration within functions as three of the eight driving forces that correlate with financial performance. Each of these three factors requires initiative, overcoming the tendency to compete, and relationship development. The relationships that develop make available mindshare for faster learning, creative problem solving, and potential service or product innovation and result in the communication needed to "create a greater collective intelligence," according to Fitz-enz.[5] In other words, relationships enable the whole to be greater than the sum of its parts.

The time is gone when managers can do their job from behind closed doors, rely completely on their own experience or intuition, communicate via e-mail or memo, and make guest appearances at meetings. Unless you want to send the unspoken message, "You and your work don't matter—I am working on important things that I won't tell you about," you must communicate regularly with your employees, model collaboration within your department, and partner with other functions inside and outside your organization. The relationships that result from communication, collaboration, and partnering will provide a nonreproducible competitive advantage to your individual employees, your department, the organization overall—and to you.

Bonding New Hires to the Organization

Relationship building begins with the first contact with the candidate and does not end even after years of working together. It is an ongoing process. You can safely assume that all your job candidates are engaged in an active job search. You must set your organization apart through immediate relationship building with all potential candidates. You can see how one company accomplished that task in "What's Working" on pages 136–137. Too few organizations respond politely (or at all) to candidates, or even to those selected for interviews. Ask your HR partner whether an automated e-mail response is feasible. Conscious relationship building on your part will add positive polish to your organization's employment brand.

What's Working at JW Marriott

The key to successfully hiring and managing off-site employees, says Jane M. Chaney, CMP, director of marketing for JW Marriott Orlando, Grande Lakes, is "caring about the individual and keeping remote employees 'top of mind.' Like Mr. Marriott says, 'If you take care of your employees, they will take care of the customer.'" Her positive track record with "remote" employees is one that other managers of choice can duplicate.

To find great sales manager candidates in other cities, she targets top competitors by calling Marriott hotels in those cities to ask, "If you lose a business opportunity, who gets it?" She also calls professional organizations—in this case, meeting planners—to ask, "Who handles your account with the top hotels? If you had to hire one or more of these sales managers, who would you hire, and why? And, who takes the best care of you?"

Once candidates are identified, Ms. Chaney says, a three-stage process including different types of telephone interviews is conducted prior to a final face-to-face interview.

> In stage one, I conduct the first screening telephone interview. My vice president and general manager do the next-level interviews followed by having two potential peers interview the sales manager candidate. The best candidates move to stage two: a forty-five-minute Quality Selection Process (QSP) telephone interview conducted by a trained professional from Talent Plus. We use the QSP to hire all employees, from gardeners to housekeepers to sales managers, against a success profile. Stage three is the face-to-face interview in Orlando with the two final candidates.

> [Once a remote employee has been hired,] we learn what he or she feels is important. One might be touchy-feely and want a personal relationship, while another is driven, self-motivated, and "all business." It is important to help every new hire through technology issues and other obstacles so that they can get off to a good start. Weekly, we teleconference with the remote sales managers for the sales meeting, and make sure that they get the

What's Working at JW Marriott cont'd

minutes from the 8:00 a.m. daily lineup meeting we have here in the Orlando office. Our remote employees can access Web-based training so they can follow along with Orlando-based training classes, and we e-mail our PowerPoint training modules so they can follow along while teleconferenced into group training that we do weekly. Twice a year, we have a two-day sales retreat to increase team building. We also have a "go-to" person, our destination sales executive, who is available to our remote employees at all times. She answers questions about process and procedures and handles the needs of their customers coming to Orlando. The remote sales managers also come to Orlando periodically with top customers on site visits.

It is easier to have everyone on-site, but with a little extra effort remote positions work well, especially when they are "in-market" where our customers are. . . . The keys are to hire well by identifying strong focus, discipline, competition, and "positivity" talent; always include remote employees in communication; treat all employees fairly and with respect; and be flexible by giving each employee the type of relationship and work environment that makes him or her productive. Being a remote employee is not for everyone.

Manage for Retention Before Day One

There are numerous ways for you to build relationships with potential new hires, between great candidates and their potential peers, and between candidates and your organization overall. Some of these include the following:

- Return voicemails and e-mails promptly—whether from job candidates or employees.

- Listen to candidates when they mention interesting life experiences, hobbies, or accomplishments so that you can provide appropriate information when making introductions to talented potential peers.

- Ask your staff to interview top candidates, making sure that they have the updated job description to review prior to the interview. Encourage them to respond honestly to candidate questions. Give your staff's substantiated opinions equal or greater weight than your own; seek the receptionist's opinion of the candidate, too.

- Use a courier, UPS, or FedEx to deliver the offer letter tucked in a book on a topic of interest to the prospective hire; a variation could be to send the offer letter with enclosed tickets for a movie or a certificate for dinner for two so that the individual can discuss the offer with a significant other.

- Block your calendar on the expected start date once the offer is accepted.

- Send benefits paperwork to the new hire for completion in advance of the first day; coordinate with your HR partner if necessary.

- Meet with your staff to plan their roles in assimilating the new employee. Ask questions such as, "What would have made your first two weeks easier?" Ask each employee to schedule a lunch and/or a one-hour meeting with the new hire during week one.

- Select a mentor or buddy for the new hire; ask that person to keep the master calendar and checklist of welcoming activities.

- Move peer relationships forward. Schedule a breakfast or other low-key get-together that includes the new hire prior to day one. Ask your employees what they would like to do.

- Order all badges, nameplates, parking passes, welcome signs, and so on for delivery prior to day one.

- Clean and set up the new person's work area.

- Schedule the new employee's review of equipment operation and any necessary skills training (sexual harassment avoidance, computer skills, voicemail, online calendaring, instant messaging, etc.).

- Ask your staff to plan a fun social event for sometime during the new hire's first two weeks. A scavenger hunt using a "getting to know you" question list and digital camera could be a good way to help the newcomer remember names and faces, while a pitch-in lunch with some "getting to know you" team-building activities and prizes would be memorable. Reward all employees for learning more about each other during this time of assimilation.

The addition of a new person should enhance the work experience for your existing employees. Your staff is the key to the new employee's speedy assimilation. Even a great relationship with you cannot substitute for a poor relationship with peers. The new hire needs great relationships from the start to accelerate to full productivity.

Relationship Building During Orientation

Prevent your new hire from experiencing "buyer's remorse": borrow from the best practices of prominent employers of choice to ensure that relationships are positive right from the start. Whether orientation takes half a day or even several weeks, the new hire cannot be thrown to the wolves when it is over. Even the most seasoned new hire will need a multistage, multifaceted orientation approach.

Your role as manager is critical here—without a good relationship with you, the new employee will find it difficult to impossible to bond with the group or the organization overall. Instead, he or she will "fake it" until another job offer comes along. Plan to spend extra time with the new employee for several weeks. Orientation is critical to long-term retention. If available, use a combination of high-tech as well as "high-touch" processes. Do not rely on technology alone for orientation—nothing is colder. Consider the following twelve steps:

1. Be there! Your presence and participation on day one says, "Only you will do! We are glad you are here!" Your absence shouts, "Anyone with a good resume could have filled this position." Your other employees will take their cue from you and either take time with or ignore the new person accordingly.

2. Use technology to speed benefits sign-up, schedule training, and provide some company overview information.

3. Plan tours, introductions, and training activities that will minimize the new employee's time-to-productivity.

4. Make day one fun! Celebrate new hires—including remote teleworkers—with an effective day one orientation process. Personalized intranets, list servers, and e-mails make even off-site orientation powerful.

5. E-mail welcome messages from the CEO, senior management, and team members unable to be present to show how the organization values the new hire.

6. Use conference calls and videoconference meetings to make the welcome warmer. Integrate video clips from your organization's intranet into the orientation.

7. Connect your new hire with a mentor, buddy, or even e-mail counseling to minimize the overwhelming nature of a new job.

8. Videotape live orientation presentations for new hires who cannot attend in person.

9. Use checklists for the employee as well as for yourself to ensure that all orientation information is covered within the first week.

10. Survey your new hire for comments and ideas for improving the orientation process.

11. Re-survey the new employee after 3–4 weeks to ensure he or she is still on track.

12. Ask the new employee to be a buddy to your next new hire.

One of the best ways to sustain a positive relationship is to ensure that each employee is committed from the start.[6] Executing a specific plan to quickly assimilate new hires increases the odds of bonding them to you, to their peers, and to the organization. As a result, new hires will be more likely to openly communicate difficulties, interpret motives and intentions benignly, and use constructive conflict resolution strategies as necessary.

Demonstrate Inclusion Management for All Employees

Inclusive managers are the human bridges to maximum productivity. Extend inclusion to all employees, no matter what their tenure with the organization, work arrangement, or other diversity dimension. Here are a few ground rules that can be posted and discussed:

- Respect the opinions of others

- Listen without interrupting

- Avoid making judgments

- Respect confidentiality

- Participate fully—share your thoughts

- Keep group discussions on track

- Expect to feel uncomfortable at times

- Keep your sense of humor

The most powerful, positive thing you can do to demonstrate support for your employees is to give credit, affirm remarks, and refer to an employee's successes in a group meeting or group e-mail. The key is to mention the names of several employees in each meeting or throughout the month. Your comments say, "This is someone you should get to know." Make sure that you are sincere, logical, and fair and that every employee gets to bask in the positive spotlight every month. Here are some examples:

- "Tameka, you had an idea in our earlier one-on-one meeting that is worth sharing with the group."

- "Ling, take five minutes to tell your new colleagues how you solved the XYZ problem at your old employer."

- "Sheryl, tell the group what you did for the client to renew our contract without putting it out for bid."

- "Ahmed, briefly tell us why you think the project needs to be rescoped."

Keep a file of your employees' accomplishments and creative ideas so that you are ready to praise several of them appropriately at every meeting or group e-mail opportunity. Rotate the spotlight. Leave no one out.

The Power of Stereotypes, Symbols, and Words

Working for your organization is a voluntary activity. The symbols (including such things as photos, awards, buttons, and so on), words, and tone that you use guide how employees think about you, their peers, the organization, the field they are in, and even the industry. Symbols and words are part of the culture, and part of relationship building. Stereotypes can too easily creep into tone, gestures, and actions and perhaps be implied by the omission of praise.

How do you refer to your employees? Are they team members and associates—or are they subordinates and "others"? Do your words convey respect and high regard? Do you habitually introduce employees to colleagues from other departments? Do you permit a hostile environment, or do you quash racist, ethnic, ageist, sexist, or gay-bashing jokes? Be consistent and hold everyone accountable. It is the law, and it is the ethical thing to do.

What does the appearance of your department convey? Walk through your department's work areas with new eyes. Look at your own office for symbols. If this seems too difficult, look into a small mirror to see the work area as a reflection. Do you really have a cot hidden on end behind your door? Do you see the personal items, baby pictures, photos of company events, posted invitations to group get-togethers, and so on that telegraph group cohesion and the acceptance of each employee as a whole person? If you see no personal items, but do see inappropriate cartoons or photos, or if bulletin boards post legal notices and purely work-centric memos, it is unlikely that your department has a positive employment brand within the organization. Managers and departments that ignore the importance of symbols and words and their role in developing relationships inside and outside the department will struggle to attract top talent.[7]

Asking and Listening: Your Best Relationship Development Tools

Leaders listen, while "empty suits" pontificate. A 2001 Gallup poll found that employees who are "heard" are more likely to devote full energy to their jobs, but less than 50 percent of respondents reported that they receive regular feedback from their supervisors about their work performance.[8] Asking questions and listening to your employees' and peers' responses are your most powerful relationship-building tools. Ask your employees individually what matters to them, how they want to be recognized, and what symbols and behaviors are seen as positive—and which are seen as negative. Recheck these over time, as the meaning of symbols can change.

Assuming that your employees turn in weekly reports with their accomplishments, the status of projects, next week's meetings and goals, and ideas to improve workflow, sales, or cost controls, you still need a standing weekly or biweekly individual meeting. If your employees can count on having your undivided attention on a regular basis, they are less likely to interrupt you for consultation or dozens of mini-meetings. Mondays or Tuesdays are good days to block off for standing individual meetings. These meetings also minimize the likelihood of "surprises" later in the course of a project. According to Catherine Mercer Bing and Lionel Laroche in a paper on virtual teams, "identifying the solutions early—when problems remain small—can mean the difference between failure and success."[9] This is the case for all teams as well as individual employees.

Individual meetings can last for twenty minutes to an hour. Select the length most appropriate to your employees ahead of time. Close the door, if you have one; meet away from the group if you must. If you are holding consecutive short meetings, allow some time in between in case one meeting runs a few minutes longer—so as not to keep other employees waiting. Make sure that your employees can see a clock; position a second clock where you can glimpse it without it being noticed. Obvious clock watching on your part could cut off valuable communication. If employees know they will need extra time, ask them to request it in advance, or you can schedule a continuation later in the day or ask for additional information to be e-mailed to you. Unless there is a true emergency (such as the sudden resignation of top talent), stay on schedule. For off-site employees, augment e-mailed reports with more personal telephone meetings or perhaps a computer camera and the Internet.

Open-ended questions provide you with the most information. Be sure to ask the "Big Three" questions, in order:

- **"How are *you*?"** Watch and listen to the response. You need to be able to tell the difference between someone who has been up half the night with a teething child and someone who has become disconnected from the organization and has one foot out the door. If the employee is going through a tough situation at home, take a few minutes to brainstorm what they need to keep an even keel. Would a more flexible temporary schedule help? Is talking with HR or your employee assistance program (EAP) provider in order? Demonstrate caring without trying to solve the personal problem yourself. If there is a problem at work, dig into it immediately.

- **"How is the team doing?"** Again, watch and listen. You need to wear your best poker face and use open-ended questions for eliciting more information such as, "Really?" and, "Why do you think that happened?" Ask for solutions or options. Gauge the situation by what you hear and whether you hear similar input from others in the department. Your goals are to allow a bit of steam release and to guide the employee to his or her own solutions while listening for those situations that only you can resolve before they become true problems. If your staff needs energizing and more fun to offset a big backlog of work, encourage them to plan something during the week. Pizza, ice cream, duckpin bowling, a softball game, or getting to leave work two hours early on Friday can work wonders. Why not set up a softball game with the department you work with most? If your staff needs better conflict resolution skills, move quickly to get them training. Tuck training messages into your e-mails, group meetings, shared articles, and so on regularly. Practice the skills with them.

- **"How can I help you to do a better job?"** Once again, watch and listen. Brainstorm options. Respond immediately to reasonable requests. Find a way to respond positively even to unusual requests.

Your individual relationships with your employees will keep levels of morale and performance high (as illustrated in "What's

What's Working at Deloitte & Touche

"When the pressure is on managers, and they are in 'workhorse' mode, it can be a struggle to exhibit soft skills," says Bill Bagley, human resources and recruiting director with Deloitte & Touche in Cincinnati.[10]

The partners recognize that what Deloitte says about itself must be congruent with what managers and partners do, so we offer many relationship-building mechanisms beyond soft skills training. We expect all employees to treat each other with civility and integrity. We want to ensure that our employees agree that we deserve our repeated listing in *Fortune* magazine as one of the "100 Best Companies to Work For."

Among the tools for enhancing relationships and communication between employees and managers, Deloitte uses mentoring, anonymous online 360-degree feedback, counseling, and performance management (including setting specific relationship development goals). "Relationship development is important for all employees inside and outside Deloitte," adds Bagley.

To develop an external network for new business development, new hires put together a list of every person they have ever known in college and elsewhere. They are expected to know each person's birthday and current employer. Employees keep up with this network on an ongoing basis through lunches, phone calls, and voicemails.

Working," above). Listen for accomplishments, learning, collaboration, opportunities to partner with other departments, newly developed relationships that will facilitate doing business, and solvable problems. Ask for ideas that will improve quality or process as well as issues that could keep the group from meeting goals. Search for items that are praiseworthy—and give immediate praise. Note appropriate items for future awards and recognition. Encourage learning, teaching, patience, teamwork, helping, initiative, ideas, follow-through, and other activities that build relationships and develop the individual, team, or organization. Say "thank you" every day—for your employees' time, efforts, caring, creativity, and results.

Coaching for Relationships—and Results

Top-down management gave way to coaching when the quality movement and self-directed teams initiated the egalitarian atmosphere in many manufacturing workplaces, and the technology boom brought casual attire and a more informal approach into the office. The best coaches expect the best results from all their employees and raise the performance bar by focusing on the development of specific skills. They use tasks and other activities that link employee effectiveness to organizational goals. The art of coaching, however, involves walking a fine line between offering too much advice and not offering enough. Here are some tips on being a good coach:

- **Communicate goals clearly.** When setting goals, include the context and answer the question "Why?" so that employees can learn. Whether communicating verbally or in writing, always ask for questions—and take the time to answer them graciously.

- **Ask open-ended questions to clarify the situation.** Avoid yes-or-no answers by asking open-ended questions such as, "How much progress has been made so far?" "What happened next?" "What have you tried?" "Why do you think it did not/will work?" or, "What information or tools do you need?" Try not to pressure employees, but encourage them to brainstorm both practical and wild ideas.

- **Encourage individual development.** Be proactive about development plans and keep moving them forward. All your employees bring special gifts to their job. Build on their strengths. Ask for alternative courses of action without offering comments. Ask, "What is your next step?" Then ask for a commitment.

- **Recognize performance weekly or more often.** Provide fast feedback, both for what needs improvement and for praise.[11]

- **Ensure that your employees learn and grow.** Bored employees are not creative employees. Make sure that your employees are marketable within your organization so that they will not seek development or another career elsewhere. All employees need both hard skills and soft skills training at least annually. Set an expectation for continuous learning. Remove barriers to learning. Use every means possible to develop bench strength: mentoring, e-learning, CD-ROMs, cross-training, job shadowing, "lunch and learn" sessions, book and article discussions, stretch assignments, and so on. At group meetings, ask every employee to share something that he or she has learned since the last meeting.

- **Evaluate individual performance regularly.** You can set up your own meetings throughout the year for project debriefing, quality checks, and so on. Don't wait until formal annual reviews to provide feedback. Gather input from the employee and others so that a balanced review can be provided. A formal review should not be late or a surprise.

- **Show you care about your people.** Connect with, celebrate with, congratulate, cajole, and communicate with each member of your staff. If your staff includes members from unfamiliar cultures, learn about those cultures so that you can literally "appreciate where they are coming from." Make eye contact and block all calls so you can give your undivided attention in individual meetings. Ask about employees' weekend, sons' and daughters' sports, parents' health, travel plans, hobbies, and so on. Mark your calendar so that you can mention birthdays, anniversaries, and other "red letter" days.

Correct Bad Conduct Immediately

If great relationships are the fuel for employee productivity and passion, poor relationships due to a few rotten apples can spoil the communication and productivity of an otherwise dynamic group. While 10 percent of employees cause 80 percent of the performance problems,[12] every manager faces inappropriate behavior at one time or another. Bad conduct cannot be ignored. Instead, respond with the following steps:

1. **Counsel the employee.** Offer help with whatever is bothering him or her.

2. **Set expectations.** Specify appropriate behavior. Younger or foreign-born employees especially may not fully know what appropriate business behavior is. Late arrival at work and meetings, disrespectful responses to peers, eye-rolling, snickers, offensive jokes, inappropriate attire, cursing, explosive anger, sexual innuendo, drinking too much at company events, and so on can become major problems because these are behaviors that can spread to other employees. As a group, develop workplace rules, post them, and discuss them.

3. **Treat inappropriate behavior as a performance issue.** Explain how inappropriate behavior affects performance. Require harassment prevention and other training for all employees upon hiring and repeat the training annually. Frequently reinforce company and departmental rules.

4. **Refer the employee to your employee assistance program (EAP).** You are not a trained social worker or psychologist—experts are available.

5. **Follow disciplinary steps.** Don't assume that you know what to do. Contact your Human Resources partner to ensure that you are following appropriate progressive disciplinary steps and providing appropriate documentation.

6. **Monitor for improvement.** Praise employees whose behavior improves. Consider transferring or reconfiguring the work locations of employees with a specific problem who are otherwise valuable. Do not tolerate employees whose behavior does not consistently improve.

7. **Terminate the employee.** If other options have been exhausted, termination may be necessary. Consult your HR partner first.

MOCs do not ignore inappropriate behavior. They know it destroys relationships and is a morale and productivity killer. It saps mindshare and heartshare energy and will not go away by itself. Other employees may see your lack of response as a green light to mimic it. An MOC will not permit cultural norms, company rules, or the law to be violated. As soon as possible, speak to the offending employee in private. Your immediate response can get an otherwise valuable employee back on track.

Use Technology to Build Relationships

Nothing can really substitute for face-to-face communication, but "face time" is not always an option. Technology offers alternatives, though many consider it a mixed blessing.

On the plus side, technology can augment a warm relationship (such as a voicemail that tells an employee, "I appreciate everything that you are doing to get the Feensterman account closed. Your presentation showed the extra effort you have been putting in. You are a great role model for the younger sales reps."). Users can also access information through e-mail, intranets, portals, and websites at a convenient time nearly anywhere in the world. Technology can eliminate the need for some travel and meetings, thus reducing time away from the office and family, as well as reducing costs.

On the negative side, technology can also make a lukewarm relationship turn to ice (such as an e-mail that says, "Shelly did not like the ending to the videotape at all. Please call her."). It can also increase miscommunication because the sender cannot adjust the message in response to the verbal and nonverbal signals of the recipient. Plus, technology upgrades are happening so fast that "early adopters" rarely get more than a few weeks to show off the latest, smallest, multifunction high-tech accessory before the next one comes along. MOCs keep up with technology advances.

MOCs use technology to build relationships, not diminish them. As a manager, you need to use the technology that is used by your employees (see "Accelerating Relationship Building with IM" on page 152). Uniformity is an issue: differing technology use is dividing departments and organizations by generations. According to a 2002 Pew Internet & American Life Project survey, 85 percent of college students own their own computer, and more than 65 percent of college students have more than one e-mail address. More than 25 percent of college students use instant messaging every day.[13] When they become your new hires, they will bring their technology use with them to your department.

Managers must also adjust to business needs for technology security and for record keeping of all messages. Etiquette for e-mail, voicemail, cell phones, PDAs, instant messaging, and other multifunction technology is evolving. Cross-generational, cross-cultural, and even cross-organizational etiquette expectations and differences can be marked. Group discussions about protocols, timeliness of responses, shared understanding of abbreviations, acronyms, and so on are necessary to minimize miscommunication.

Use Technology to Ensure Communication up the Organization

Even the best relationships have secrets, but in business, untold secrets can cause people to leave or to assume that their best is not appreciated. Create a way for communication to occur so that you can handle questions and concerns before they become ugly rumors or you read about them in an exit interview report. Following are a few tools you can use to keep the communication lines up.

Accelerating Relationship Building with IM

In many organizations, instant messaging (IM) is almost entirely replacing the telephone, and voicemail is transforming phones into "store and forward" devices similar to e-mail. Less time consuming than waiting for e-mail or voicemail responses, IM increases productivity. Because IM is portable and can be accessed via cell phone or PDA (not just online), it is much faster than e-mail, which requires the recipient to log on or to use the telephone, both of which require recipients to be at their desk. IM enables people to work anywhere—not just at their desk. It is used for tasks that require an immediate response such as quick questions and organizing impromptu meetings.

Gartner Group predicts that IM will be used by 90 percent of North American corporations by 2004. If you are not using IM on at least a limited basis, you are falling out of the loop. Your employees have 50–200 names on their "buddy" lists—and your name should be one of them! Your wireless carrier offers pocket-sized booklets to help you "get texting." Learn the lingo and start making your presence known. IM shorthand for busy users includes the following:

IMHO   In my humble opinion
AFAIK   As far as I know
YMMV   Your mileage may vary (buyer beware)
TPTB   The powers that be
TYIA   Thank you in advance
TTYL   Talk to you later

- **Anonymous e-mail or telephone hotlines for all employees.** These allow employees and managers to post questions and messages for responses. Managers can use anonymous e-mail to ask employees for input about policies, procedures, or other problems that if not explained or changed could possibly cause them to leave. Employees can use either e-mail or the telephone hotline to check information, ask questions, report ethics violations, or share concerns. As appropriate, managers or other individuals should respond to questions and correct misinformation. Since it is safe to assume that 95 percent of questions asked are shared by many other employees, post the response in a public place such as the employee newsletter or a special bulletin board.

- **"Red Card–Yellow Card" or similar phrase in e-mail subject lines or voicemail.** This signal can be used to get the immediate attention of management concerning individual employees' issues that could either cause them to leave (red card) or harm the organization's reputation and/or relationships (yellow card). Employees at all levels can use this process to communicate upward—but it can start with you and your department! When a regularly scheduled meeting would require too long a wait, employees need an alternative way to convey the seriousness of a concern. Always welcome employees to see you immediately and thank them for making the effort early so that you have a chance to solve the problem. Any dismissive gestures or words that indicate that the issue is not worthy of immediate attention will send the message throughout the organization that the early warning system is broken. The alternative will become failure to communicate an issue that results in turnover or other harm to the organization.

- **Counseling pairs and other formalized interventions.** These tools are used in many organizations to minimize the possibility of turnover. Trained employees are available as confidential facilitators and intermediaries on behalf of employees who are concerned about the breakdown of their relationship with their manager. The use of such a tool signals significant communication and trust issues in need of repair.

- **Open forums—with or without the use of technology.** Let employees talk about what is important to them. Their goal is to be heard. If you chair an open forum, expect initial meetings to contain a lot of general griping. Take notes, remain open, and respond as quickly and publicly as possible so that future meetings become more substantive and productive. Be sure to ask employees why they think the problem is occurring. Ask for their suggestions for solutions. Over time, the meetings will evolve into joint problem-solving sessions. Your employees will collaborate with you on solutions.

Technology for Virtual and Blended Teams

Technology is both the enabler and the bond for virtual teams (whose members never meet due to time zone or other distances) and blended teams (made up of some people who may physically work together and others who are off-site). To speed and reinforce relationship development and to develop trust among teams in complex projects,

- Hold a preliminary meeting to outline protocols that participants can agree on: regularly scheduled meetings, delineation of responsibilities, etc.

- Be sensitive to meeting times that repeatedly inconvenience the same people—consider alternating times or dates if no mutually convenient times can be found for the entire group

- E-mail or physically mail around photos of team members with short bios so that everyone gets to "meet" everyone else, even if it is on paper. Ask the team what they want to know about each other. Don't be surprised if questions about children and hobbies augment questions about work experiences.

- Send agendas at least one day prior to videoconference or teleconference meetings

- If possible, use videoconferencing (not just teleconferencing) for at least some meetings. Prepare team members to expect a lag between the spoken word and the heard word. Extroverts may need to be reminded to ask each team member for input. Do not let team members remain silent for the entire meeting.

- Use instant messaging to automatically notify team members when one team member is on the Internet, and to allow them to simultaneously exchange e-mails

- Use an electronic bulletin board to post questions and collect comments

- Use Web-based team measurement tools to collect team interactions; e-mail minutes or reports to every team member

- Augment regular meetings with opportunities to socialize

Tying It All Together

Relationships are two-way, so communication needs to be two-way. Take the "relationship temperature" of your department on Monday morning. How do your employees greet each other? Do they share weekend stories? Are they happy to see each other? If not, it is time to rev up the relationships and the energy of the group through fun team-building events. Consult your HR partner or resources at the end of this chapter for ideas.

Your employees do not have to be "best buds"—but they do have to cooperate, help each other, and know each other beyond the work at hand. Otherwise, every day is just a day of tasks and transactions that are available anywhere. Team building on a small scale every week can go far to improve group performance and create a foundation for synergistic thinking.

Be ready to recognize your employees' relationship development efforts. The easy parts will include socializing or ensuring that the right people are included. There are harder elements, too.

Employees must be willing to apologize if they have said anything to damage their work relationships. They find it easier to do if they have heard you do the same. Create recognition programs for the best relationship builders as determined by their peers.

MOCs ask and listen, credit others publicly, are curious and open-minded even when confronted with input believed to be untrue, and use relationships to build better employees, departments, organizations, and communities. As Bruce Tulgan says, retaining the best people will have to happen "one person at a time, one day at a time, on the basis of ongoing negotiation."[14] To have your employees' heartshare, mindshare, and mutual trust is to have a strong relationship indeed!

Discussion Questions

1. What behaviors signal that someone is not listening? Are some behaviors considered rude by some ethnic, age, or other groups but not by others? Do you include all these behaviors in discussions about etiquette and values?

2. Do you have regularly scheduled weekly or biweekly meetings with each of your direct reports? If not, look at your calendar to see what blocks of time can be set aside for regular meetings and let your employees choose their preferred time slots. Ask that written or e-mailed reports be turned in the day before the meeting (on Friday for Monday meetings) so that you have a chance to look them over in advance. It will take only a few weeks for everyone to get into the rhythm of regular meetings.

3. What questions do you plan to ask your employees during this week's weekly meeting? How can you use questions to boost their self-esteem and further develop needed skills?

4. Do you believe that technology is enhancing your relationships with each of your employees, their relationships with each other, other departments, and the outside community? Schedule a lunch meeting to ask employees to suggest how to better use technology to improve communication and relationships. Provide snacks and beverages and ask all to attend.

Resources

To learn more about coaching, relationship development, and being a great people manager, read:

The Boss's Survival Guide by Bob Rosner, Allan Halcrow, and Alan Levins. New York: McGraw-Hill, 2001.

Bridging the Boomer-Xer Gap by Hank Karp, Connie Fuller, and Danilo Sirias. Palo Alto, CA: Davies-Black Publishing, 2002.

Creating Commitment by Michael N. O'Malley. New York: John Wiley and Sons, 2000.

Fast Feedback by Bruce Tulgan. Amherst, MA: HRD Press, 1999.

First Among Equals: How to Manage a Group of Professionals by Patrick J. McKenna and David H. Maister. New York: The Free Press, 2002.

Winning the Talent Wars by Bruce Tulgan. New York: W. W. Norton and Company, 2001.

"Communication Technologies for Virtual Teams" by Catherine Mercer Bing and Lionel Laroche. *OD Practitioner* 34, 2 (2002).

"The Diversity Executive: Tasks, Competencies, and Strategies for Effective Leadership," The Conference Board, Inc., New York, NY, Council Report R-1300-01-CR, www.conferenceboard.org, 2001.

Trust Builder

"If you want innovation, you must not only accept risk and mistakes, you must demand them."

—**Jac Fitz-enz,** *The 8 Practices of Exceptional Companies*[1]

As a manager of choice (MOC), you have two ongoing tasks: building trust with job candidates and new employees and strengthening or rebuilding trust with existing staff, peers, and senior management. For managers, trust building is a Sisyphean endeavor: trust must be re-earned every day. And, it can be lost in a single moment of anger or deceit. The best managers are the best trust builders.

How important is trust in your workplace? To answer this, you need to look at the public's perception of your organization's brand—its product/service brand and its employment brand—and at your "personal brand" as an MOC. Trust in your organization's product or service brand determines whether your products or services are purchased. It determines whether vendors compete for your business, banks want to extend credit to you, and other individuals and organizations want to do business with you. Similarly, trust in your organization's employment brand determines whether job seekers feel positive about applying and whether the organization as a whole gets cooperation and enthusiastic participation from employees.

Trust in your personal brand is determined by the effect of your daily words and actions. To engender trust in current employees, hire carefully, sparingly, and well to ensure that new hires are likely to succeed. Share abundant information, encourage creativity, and forgive mistakes. Add the benefits of challenging work to stretch employee capabilities and competitive pay that includes regular rewards and recognition as part of the compensation package. In return, you can expect the very best thinking, decisions, and effort from each employee at every level. When you, as the representative of your organization, give the best, you can expect the best. Trust is reciprocal.

In this chapter we look at the current state of trust, how MOCs build trust through deliberate modeling of the organization's values and continuous communication, and the importance of trust as the enabler for positive work–life balance programs.

Trust Is Key for Companies on the "100 Best Companies to Work For" List

To support the increasingly complex and interrelated products and services provided by today's organizations, considerable cooperation among work groups is needed. This requires trust among employees and between employees and the organization's management. The Great Place to Work® Institute zeros in on trust when they evaluate organizations for the "100 Best Companies to Work For" list published annually in *Fortune* magazine. Their Trust Index® survey is used to measure input from 250 randomly selected employees on fifty-five statements. It is the employees' responses, not the company's self-nomination, that determines inclusion on this prestigious employer of choice list.

Table 7 The Role of Trust in the Workplace	
	Credibility • Communications open and accessible • Competence in coordinating human and material resources • Integrity in carrying out vision with consistency
	Respect • Supporting professional development and showing appreciation • Collaboration with employees on relevant decisions • Caring for employeees as individuals with personal lives
	Fairness • Equity—balanced treatment for all in terms of rewards • Impartiality—absence of favoritism in hiring and promotions • Justice—lack of discrimination and a process for appeals
	Pride • In personal job, individual contributions • In work produced by one's team or work group • In the organization's products and standing in the community
	Camaraderie • Ability to be oneself • Socially friendly and welcoming atmosphere • Sense of "family" or "team"

© 2002 Great Place to Work® Institute, Inc. All rights reserved. Reprinted with permission.

According to Scott Cawood, Ph.D., of the Great Place to Work® Institute's East Coast office, "Innovations require an environment where people feel they can go beyond what they have done in the past. We have a considerable body of research that demonstrates that organizations with higher levels of trust are superior performers in terms of productivity and profitability." The institute's list of ways that trust is played out in the workplace is shown in table 7. As you review the table, think about the people in your department. Where would they rank you in fostering trust in each of those five work dimensions?

Organizations need cultures with 360-degree trust for information to flow and for performance to remain consistently high. Two-way trust between an employee and a manager becomes 360-degree trust when it also exists among employees, among managers, and between senior managers and their staffs. Trusting individuals communicate, and communicators can be expected to ensure higher-quality products and services. Your internal organization's trust level becomes the foundation for trust between your organization as a whole and your customers and investors.

The Status of Trust in the Workplace

Many organizations today are struggling with issues of trust. Mergers and acquisitions with attendant restructurings and downsizings exacted a high toll on trust during the eighties and nineties. After the debacles at Enron/Andersen, WorldCom, and elsewhere, trust repair continues in earnest. When local headlines say, "FBI has launched a probe of Kmart,"[2] and the internationally focused *Economist* magazine cover features headlines such as "The Wickedness of Wall Street," trust in big business is so low that all it can do is go up.[3] This is critical since trust is arguably the engine for the whole capitalist system.[4]

Fortunately, trust is faring better within individual organizations than the global headlines would indicate. A Gallup/UBS Employee Outlook poll of workers in for-profit companies found that 86 percent have a great deal or a moderate amount of trust in both the people who run their organization and the people who handle the finances and accounting at their company. Ninety percent of respondents said that top executives try to do what is best for the customers, 72 percent said that top executives try to do what is best for the employees, and 68 percent believe that top executives try to do what is best for stockholders.[5] How would individuals in your organization rate their trust in the company?

Trust makes the business world go round. The people who decide whether to buy your organization's products and services, as well as its stock, are just like the consumers of the work experience—your employees—who decide whether to work for you and your organization and either engage fully or "leave their brains at the door." If employees trust you and senior management, they will persuade the people they know to support your organization's growth by working there or buying the products or services. Your employees must believe and trust in you to want to bring their best ideas and energy to their work. This will determine how enthusiastically they respond to the opportunities you put before them. The higher their trust in you and in each other, the easier it will be for you to build a high-performing team.

Modeling the Organizational Values

Great managers, says David Maister, author of *Practice What You Preach*, "give lots of responsibility early, are available to help, set and enforce high standards (on things other than just financial results), demand participation by all team members, and set a high personal example."[6] As the walking, talking, living embodiment of the organization's culture, how can you expect to do anything less than model the core values?

Trust is the key to the employee–manager relationship and correlates strongly with retention.[7] Organizations with high trust scores have employees who perceive they can trust their managers, team members, and the organization to keep promises, follow through on commitments, and provide accurate information when asked. In a survey of 655 employees conducted by Linkage, Inc., of Lexington, Massachusetts, the top four factors that influence employee retention are

- Trust

- Organizational values

- Perceived value of the individual

- Communication between departments

As a manager, you are central to all four factors. Employees of any generation, race, religion, sexual preference, national origin, or work configuration tend to most easily trust members of the same group. Your efforts to build a relationship with each one individually, and among the staff as a group, will pay off in elevated trust levels.

Your employees were attracted to your organization because they heard it was a terrific place to work. In the interview process, you and every element of the process were tested for "matching" against the external messages that make up your organization's brand. Your employees represent a mass of people power, but they want to be managed individually—not as members of a category. What it will take to build trust with each person may differ a bit, but it all comes down to matching: Does the way you talk and act match up with your organization's brand (the reputation of its products/services plus customer experiences with them), and does the employment brand (employee experiences) align with the published organizational values?

As an example of how daily operations can conflict with the organization brand and employment brand, consider the recent stonewalling of senior management at Bridgestone/Firestone when they were presented with reports of widespread tire defects in the 1990s. Most organizations' stated values include customer service and integrity. How would years of refusal to take responsibility for complaints from injured drivers and passengers as well as dealerships and insurance companies match up with those values? How did stonewalling strengthen or increase employee morale, productivity, quality, the ability to recruit, business partnerships, or sales? Of course it had the opposite effect. Incongruity of actions and statements with organizational values decreases trust. Lower trust damages relationships, performance, and the bottom line.

What are your organization's stated values? Are they posted in your workspace? If not, post them! Are they posted in your department? If not, post them! Have you ever taken the values one at a time as discussion items in department meetings? If not, do it—and ask employees to do it, too. Your employees can take each value and determine how they can conduct their own responsibilities in a way that confirms it. Ask your employees how you can better "walk the talk" of organizational values. Ask if there is anything that you do or say that seems incongruous with the organization's values. Discuss these items and do all that you can to avoid repeating them. As in all things, intent is nice, but perception is reality. Make your positive intentions align with your employees' experiences and perceptions.

Improving Trust Levels in Your Department

Trust is your department's competitive advantage. As a manager, it is your individual competitive advantage as well and a key factor in whether you are seen as an MOC. No one but you can build employees' trust in you; no one but you can tear it down. According to research by Dennis Raina and Michelle Raina,[8] the three elements of trust are

- **Competency:** trust in experience and educational background

- **Contractual:** trust in what someone does

- **Communication:** trust in what someone says

Your experience as represented by your title as manager by itself is not enough to engender trust. What you do and what you say are necessary to complete the picture. It is not uncommon for someone with an otherwise sterling background to negate trust through their words or actions. A micro-manager who questions every expense despite adequate documentation or a team-building specialist who gossips both destroy trust—perhaps forever. Of course,

Five Ways to Rebuild Trust

Everyone makes mistakes or says things they would like to take back. Following are five ways to bounce back from a mistake and rebuild trust:

1. **Take responsibility.** When you are at fault, shifting blame fools no one but yourself. MOCs are not afraid to say, "I made a mistake." This recognition and an apology not only engender trust, but also make you part of the solution.

2. **Communicate your solution.** Reestablish credibility by stating what you did, what you are doing about it, and what you learned.

3. **Ask for advice.** Your own manager, peers, and employees will be impressed with your response so far, but you can take it one step further by asking them how you can avoid making the mistake in the future.

4. **Use appropriate nonverbal communication.** Be aware that confident, open body language and good eye contact help to build trust. Arms crossed over your chest, half-hearted handshaking, or lack of eye contact send negative signals.

5. **Give before you get.** Give trust first and you are more likely to receive it. Since trust is reciprocal, initiate the reciprocity. Give something of value such as a sincere "thank you," an idea, time off, a spot bonus, or even just focused attention, and increased trust will be returned.

---

all managers make mistakes, but they apologize, continually seek to improve—and they talk about it. A list of ways to rebuild trust is presented above.

The Trust–Performance Link

Trust plays a central role in your employees' daily performance, according to Thad Green, author of *Motivation Management.* Too often, managers "consistently give employees what they deserve for poor performance, but do nothing when performance is good. This creates a trust problem."[9] Green's application model, the Belief System of Motivation and Performance™, explains how employees determine how hard they will work and how well they will perform. Their effort leads to performance, which leads to outcomes, which result in satisfaction.

According to Green's model as summarized here, trust is one of three beliefs that form the foundation of desired employee performance outcomes:

1. **Confidence.** Given a project or task, employees ask, "*Can* I do it?" Your employees must believe that the effort they are capable of giving will be sufficient to perform as expected. Do your employees believe?

2. **Trust.** Assuming employees have confidence, they ask, "Will rewards be tied to my performance?" Employees must trust that you will provide rewards as promised and as their performance merits. Employees sense when their manager will not follow through—and when there will be no consequences to their performance one way or another. If employees do not trust that rewards are tied to their performance, then both their motivation and performance are in jeopardy.

3. **Satisfaction.** Traditionally, managers have believed that offering satisfying outcomes or rewards will produce motivation—but what is satisfying to one person may not be to another. Employees may have confidence and may trust that the reward or outcome will be tied to performance, but if the reward is not satisfying, performance will likely fall short. Often, tangible rewards may not be what is desired, while coaching, time off, praise, recognition, and fair treatment may fill the bill. Ask your employees what rewards would be satisfying to them.

Managers often fail to see the connection between motivation and performance, focusing solely on the end result, performance.

This is shortsighted. A lack of trust may need to be overcome. Uncover the barriers to performance by uncovering employees' beliefs. Their trust in you will ignite their motivation, innovation, and performance!

Trust and Success for Work–Life Balance Programs

Trust among employees and between you and individual employees can be a challenge in today's changing workplace. You are unlikely to be able to staff your department with on-site, full-time, 9-to-5 employees because fewer employees are finding the traditional structure attractive, and the lack of high-quality candidates will require organizations and individual managers to offer creative arrangements. Different life stages may influence your employees' preferences for full-time, part-time, telework, job-sharing, project, shift, or other work configurations. Some employees, for example, may want to work full-time for seven to nine months a year and then not at all for the remaining months. Others may want part-time telecommuting, while still others may have the time for only one day a week of high-impact contribution. Getting the work done the best way will require finding the best people and fitting the work to them, not the other way around.

Your employees' desire to fit work around life (whether family, school, or other jobs) instead of fitting life around work are fueling increased requests for work–life balance and flexibility. But, if your organization has historically placed managers and employees in close physical proximity, how will you know that work is actually being accomplished if some or all of your employees are off-site? How will your other employees know? Trust combined with regular communication and reporting should make this possible. The efforts of a University of California campus are described in "What's Working" on page 169. Getting past spoken or unspoken objections by on-site personnel to "special treatment" can require extraordinary trust and communication. It is critical to set and

What's Working at University of California, Davis[10]

Being a large employer in a small community can be a challenge. Since 40 percent of the faculty and staff will retire in the next few years, the university expects to have an increasingly younger employee population—and an increasing need for work–life balance programs. Repeated needs assessments, for example, have revealed a real need for childcare subsidies. The administration has made work–life balance programs a priority. As a result of employee requests and successful pilot programs, benefits at the university now include

- On-site childcare and kindergarten
- Breastfeeding support (10 rooms at various locations around campus for breastfeeding mothers)
- Flex-time
- Nurse on call 24 hour a day
- Alternative work schedules
- Catastrophic leave assistance (employees donate unused vacation time to assist colleagues in need)
- Broad family leave policies
- On-site athletic facilities
- On-site housing for faculty and staff
- Job placement assistance for domestic partners

Communication is the key to success. All new programs are introduced to all employees through formal and informal training sessions. Information about all programs is easily accessible through the university website. Paperwork is kept to a minimum. Programs evolve, expand, or shrink according to employee needs. "We have lower turnover and higher morale. We are seeing increased interest in people being attracted to the school," said Virginia Hinshaw, provost and executive chancellor.

communicate expectations to ensure that all in the work group know what to expect from off-site employees and that off-site employees know what support they can expect from the core group. Time is valuable to all employees, so speed of communication is essential. A combination of high tech and "high touch" will benefit everyone. Instant messaging, on-computer cameras, teleconference capabilities, or collaborative software are available at a small price. You can create a database of employees' photos and some personal information. Ask employees to recognize and reward the "super communicators" in the group. Thank individuals publicly for their efforts to use technology and regular communication to enhance trust and productivity.

Tying It All Together

"Like it or not, we do need to be good—individually—every day, day in and day out. We can't abdicate to policies, regulations or laws our personal responsibility for integrity and ethical behavior," said James E. Copeland, CEO of Deloitte & Touche.[11] Relationships build trust, and trust enables true two-way communication. The strategies that work, according to respondents in a 2001 Gallup poll include the following:[12]

- Treat employees more like partners

- Help employees to develop a "community" in their workplace

- Be proactive in developing work–life balance by offering such things as flexible hours, childcare and eldercare programs, counseling and referrals, etc.

- Promote a sense of working for a higher cause: talk about organizational values; encourage volunteering on company time

- Offer opportunities for professional development and mentoring

- Continually rebuild trust

Trust is a critical element in the flow of information. By sharing financial and performance information with your staff, you show them that you trust them to make decisions and to take the risks that lead to innovation. In the National Employee Relationship Report, a nationwide survey, trust in employees—specifically giving them the freedom to make decisions, manage their own time, control resources, and try new things—is one of the keys to improving retention.[13] MOCs keep their good people and inspire them to higher levels of performance by building trust.

Discussion Questions

1. How would you rate trust between yourself and each of your employees? Why is it higher for some than for others? What will you do to improve it?

2. Do you believe that trust is reciprocal? If so, would you agree that each of your employees trusts you as much as you trust each of them?

3. What types of behaviors cause you to trust some employees more than others? Have you spoken directly to those whom you trust less about changing those behaviors? Have you asked how you can change behaviors that are lowering your employees' trust in you?

4. What do you do to reward and recognize your on-site and off-site employees for their excellence in communication?

5. What could you do to improve trust and communication between off-site and on-site employees? What ideas do your off-site employees have for improving trust and communication with them?

Resources

To learn more about developing two-way trust, read:

Building Trust at the Speed of Change: The Power of the Relationship-Based Corporation by Edward M. Marshall. New York: Amacom, 1999.

Building Trust: A Manager's Guide for Business Success by Mary Shurtleff. Menlo Park, CA: Crisp Publications, 1998.

Motivation Management by Thad Green. Palo Alto, CA: Davies-Black Publishing, 2000.

Trust and Betrayal in the Workplace by Dennis S. Raina and Michelle L. Raina. San Francisco: Berrett-Koehler Publishers, 1999.

Skill Builder

"This is a knowledge economy, not a service economy."

—Graham Toft, senior fellow, Hudson Institute[1]

Imagine your weekly department meeting in which you provide financial and performance information and a brief training session. Your staff gets to ask questions and practice the "skill of the week." It would be a good meeting, wouldn't it? Now imagine a weekly or biweekly department meeting where you provide financial and performance information, but your employees take turns leading a brief training session or facilitating a discussion about an article or several chapters in a book that all have read. At this meeting everyone gets to ask questions, shares "one thing I learned this week," learns two more new phrases in Spanish or another language, and votes for the winner of the "Idea of the Week." This meeting would be a *great* meeting, wouldn't it?

Operational excellence can be a two-edged sword if it cuts us off from new ideas and creative things being done by distant competitors or emerging businesses. Continuous learning is required if we are to encourage innovative thinking and learn from our competitors. But, continuous learning today is not enough. Managers of choice (MOCs) engage all employees in continuous *teaching,* too. Everyone has something to share—or can learn something to share. To accelerate innovation, you must expand your employees' work world as well as accelerate skill building and knowledge for everyone on staff—including yourself. Research indicates that 20 percent of employee turnover occurs because employees feel their organization does not develop them sufficiently quickly enough.[2] MOCs triumph over turnover by developing their on-site and off-site employees—and themselves—as skill builders.

In this chapter we look at the ways MOCs weave learning into the everyday experience of the workplace using a variety of methods and source media and create an internal "free-agent nation" of movement for their employees—and develop themselves at the same time.

Ongoing Skill Building Requires Ongoing Needs Assessment

Many organizations use formal needs assessment as part of their annual planning cycle. Typically, employees and their managers are given a brief survey asking which of a list of topics correspond to their learning needs for the upcoming year. There may be an opportunity to add topics, as needed. The input is rolled up into an organization-wide training plan, and individual performance development plans are supposed to incorporate required as well as elective courses. Some organizations assemble a specific list of requirements and electives into an internal certification process for supervisors, leaders, managers, and others. In this way courses add up to a body of knowledge and skills for use by specified positions.

What skills or knowledge do your employees need? Advances in technology, global competition, and changing customer needs are external drivers of training needs. Internal organizational demographics add to the list. According to the Society for Human Resource Management's "Workplace Demographic Trends Survey," diversity is driving the need for more language, management, and recruiting training to assist different generations, races, and ethnic groups working together.[3] Respondents identified their employees' needs as follows:

- Tolerance for employees of different backgrounds (52 percent)

- Training or retraining (48 percent)

- Diversity training (41 percent)

- Bilingual communication skills (28 percent)

- Language training (27 percent)

- Sexual harassment avoidance training (22 percent)

If your organization has a formal training needs assessment process, be sure to make full use of it. Whatever the level of formal training offered by your organization, you need to augment it with content-rich, must-attend department meetings as well as other opportunities for you and your staff to learn something every day. Skill builders enable their employees to reinvent themselves. Learning generates excitement and will turn your department into a talent magnet within your organization.

Develop a Mini–Training Function in Your Department

Your organization's competitors are emerging from an expanding range of locations and types of businesses. They are focused on listening to customer needs and maximizing each employee's intellectual capital. Team up with your HR partner to discuss how you can develop a mini–training function inside your department.

Innovation is about doing things very well but differently; creativity is about dreaming up new ideas or rearranging existing ideas to meet customer demands. Being a skill builder requires both.

"Adults learn on the run," says Graham Toft, senior fellow at the Hudson Institute. "They need learning that is convenient, modular, affordable and leading to a credential or wage/job advance."[4] Twenty to thirty minutes a day keeps overall learning moving forward. Ideally, you will have an HR partner as a sounding board. If not, talk with your mentor. If you do not have a mentor or peer mentor, get one! Or, involve your staff even more in the skill-builder process. You can augment the available formal training using the following steps and tools.

Create a Learning Task Force

You can be the sponsor, but your employees need to facilitate the operation of the learning task force. If your department works closely with one or more other departments, talk to your peer managers and ask for representatives to participate in the task force. If you have external customers, invite them to participate in learning planning, too. Don't let the task force become too big—but make sure you have a cross section of up to 10–15 varied participants. Create a diverse cultural mix of men and women, hourly and salaried, long-term and short-term, on-site and off-site employees. Be sure to include some of the biggest complainers as well as some opinion leaders.

Align the Training Effort with Business Goals

Establish clear targets for the training efforts so that, together, the efforts enhance the overall department's abilities to meet its goals. Ask the task force, "What skills, behaviors, or knowledge do you need to do your jobs better and meet our business goals?" and, "What training subjects could use updating, a refresher, or more explanation?" Also ask what skills, behaviors, or knowledge you should develop to better help them to achieve their goals. If appropriate, fold your needs into their overall learning efforts; if not, find other ways to develop yourself and report results back to the group. Develop topics that can be covered in twenty- to thirty-minute segments during department meetings or covered through job shadowing and cross-training. Prioritize the topics according to which items would have the greatest or most immediate impact.

Determine the Variety of Methods and Media to Be Used
Learning should not be confined to the classroom. Mix up methods and media for maximum interest and impact. Low-cost, high-impact alternatives to classroom training sessions can enable your employees to build their skills when and where they need it. Organizations of all sizes are using the following:

- **"Lunch and learn" sessions.** This learning tool requires food and beverages, AV support, markers and flip-charts (or laptops), and an hour. A variety of formats are workable: employees can teach each other; employee peers from professional organizations can be invited to make brief presentations; new hires can be engaged in their first two weeks to select and/or present a topic they think is valuable; and top candidates for an open position can each make a twenty-minute presentation and/or facilitate a twenty-minute dialogue as part of the selection process.

- **Discussion groups.** These learning vehicles require a small budget for books, videos, and other source materials, refreshments, and an hour. A variation is to create a bookshelf library or online resource center so that employees have access to information on a variety of business and work–life balance topics. Employees could be given a book allowance to cover purchases of needed business books. Ask that all books purchased be donated to the library when the employee no longer needs them. Label donated books "From the private library of _____."

- **Job shadowing and cross-training.** These proven learning tools require one or more hours up to several days and can be handled formally or informally, but the experience must be content-rich. Job shadowing involves an experienced employee spending a typical day, or longer, with a new or otherwise inexperienced individual. One example is a "ride-along" with a new sales rep. The experience offers a variety of tasks for the newcomer to observe and discuss with the experienced employee. Cross-training involves knowledge transfer of a skill or technique. Longtime as well as newer employees often have special techniques and areas of expertise to share with others. Use job shadowing and cross-training to encourage cross-pollination of knowledge among your employees or between your employees and those in another department with whom they work closely. Sufficient cross-training greatly reduces the effect of work stoppers such as vacations, injury, and illness. As an expansion of traditional job shadowing, invite students to job-shadow your employees as a way to reach out to the community, build a pipeline of future hires, and develop your employees' mentoring and presentation skills. Go to www.jobshadow.org for everything you need to prepare for a positive student job-shadowing event.

- **Research from professional organization websites and journals, print or online newsletters, and other on- and off-line sources.** In thirty minutes or less, an employee or intern can conduct valuable research on "best practices" topics. Ask interested employees or interns to share what they learn as part of ongoing overall education in your department. Let your employees determine which articles should be shared and/or discussed in person or online, stored in a departmental library for later access, or distributed in some other way.

- **In-house or outside customer visits.** These high-impact activities require coordination with the other in-house department (your in-house "customer") or your sales department, plus AV support, refreshments, and a meeting room. In advance of the meeting, conduct a simple performance assessment of your department's interactions or services to the customer, asking, "What three things do we do well?" "What three things could we improve—and how would it help?" and, "If cost or time were no object, what would be the ideal way to work with you?" Using results from the customer input, ask the customer representative to share how the quality, quantity, and timing of your department's output affect functionality and quality requirements. Ask employees to take notes, ask questions, and start brainstorming solutions with the customer. Ask that a second brainstorming meeting be held to narrow down the final action plan. After implementation, continue the dialogue with the customer to determine whether the employee changes had the desired effect. Celebrate with a party or other form of recognition when the customer is satisfied by your employees' new skills, knowledge, and procedures.

- **Alliances with local tech schools, community colleges, and universities.** This learning approach requires tuition reimbursement and a flexible schedule arrangement if your employees are students, and only a time investment if they become guest lecturers. If your organization offers tuition reimbursement, make sure that you enable your employees to fully participate in their classes. Both school and work require time management and multitasking talents of the highest order. Encourage your student-employees to solve real business problems through their class projects and offer their services as guest lecturers, too.

- **E-learning.** This high-tech learning tool requires coordination with your HR or Training partner and a small budget. It enables a consistent presentation of real-world simulations and task-based learning to geographically diverse, multilingual, and

What's Working for E-Learning Users

E-learning makes sense since so many other business functions are moving online. E-learning can be used as a competitive differentiator to reduce costs of on-site training and orientation, enable orientation and training of off-site employees, train uniformly around the world, quickly fill knowledge gaps, accelerate new product launches, and increase customer loyalty through education and enhanced problem solving. E-learning provides training that is just-in-time, just enough, and just for you.

- **Deloitte & Touche** uses PlaceWare® to enable six-hour training sessions to be segmented over several lunch hours to train geographically dispersed consultants and other employees. Armed with a telephone and a laptop, employees can call in from a client site and participate in training using an e-mailed PowerPoint® presentation. Attendance at annual training used to be problematic due to client project conflicts, but now larger training efforts can be accomplished using lunch-hour and after-hours sessions. PlaceWare enables consultants to meet client needs and does not negatively impact utilization (billable hours), while still enabling ongoing training.[5]

- **Unisys** set its sights on being both a high-performance learning organization and an employer of choice as ways to attain a clear competitive advantage. Billable employees—both in need of ongoing training and ongoing customer contact—need a way to obtain training with less travel and training time. Unisys University teamed with SkillSoft to create e-learning to align with business needs and drive a consistent cultural message worldwide. Participants enjoy a 95 percent passing rate on certification tests. An independent employee survey conducted by International Data Corporation found that employee satisfaction increased nearly 50 percent in one year. Overall Unisys employee satisfaction jumped to 76 percent in 2000 from 29 percent in 1999. One hundred

What's Working for E-Learning Users cont'd

respondents viewed Unisys University as a competitive advantage for themselves and for Unisys. In 2000, Unisys received the Institute of IT Training Gold Award for International Training Project of the Year, as well as the Personnel Today Award for Best HR Outsourced Partnership.[6]

- **Anheuser-Busch and Harvard Business School** are two organizations that have similar systems to provide on-demand training led by the learner. The e-learning system anticipates employee needs through a process called "inference." (This is similar to the process used by www. amazon.com to recommend books based on books customers have accessed or purchased in the past.) The e-learning system recommends training and reading based on categories of information accessed by the employee. The system goes further by "pushing" articles, books, and other learning resources to the employee via e-mail. HR is able to generate reports that analyze the topics researched by employees and can then develop additional training and resources to assist.[7]

differently able employees, as described above in "What's Working." Your employees can determine needs 24/7/365, set the pace, and be tested online for learning. As needed or desired, classroom discussion can be used to reinforce difficult concepts and maximize e-learning effectiveness. One skills reinforcement combination could include e-learning and "lunch and learn" sessions.

Develop Employee Recognition and Rewards for Skill Building

All employees should be expected to learn and to teach as part of their performance management requirements. Ongoing learning and teaching positively affect your department's productivity and employability inside and outside the organization. Skill building feeds young and old minds alike with ideas that can be translated into innovation and quality. Ask your employees what types of recognition and rewards are meaningful to them. Expect an array of responses that can be used on a rotating basis for maximum effect. Be sure to use fun and experiences as rewards. Encourage employees to respond personally to their peers' training and learning efforts.

Community Involvement Is a Skill-Building Tool

Meeting new people can be a learning tool in itself. Getting your employees—and yourself—connected with a variety of community activities not only helps the community, but also pays dividends to the company, to the employees, and to you. In a study by the Points of Light Foundation and the Conference Board,[8] representatives from 2,700 companies said that volunteerism

- Improves a company's image or brand (94 percent)

- Builds employee teamwork skills (93 percent)

- Increases employee productivity (74 percent)

Think about the range of skills used and learned through most volunteer activities. Community organizations provide free training in meeting facilitation, conflict resolution, events planning, initiative, follow-through, budgeting, and so on. Community involvement builds "know-who" as well as know-how, and makes recruiting easier.

Create Your Own Free-Agent Nation

Managers spend a lot of time on turnover issues because they do not spend enough time on employee development. Without specific effort on your part to focus on skill building, your employees will not visualize themselves with your department or organization for the long term. *Free agent* is another term for *consumer of the work experience.* To your employees, internal marketability is every bit as important as external marketability, so their skill development is paramount. Up-to-date skills and abilities are their means of being selected to stay if there is a layoff or landing a new job quickly if a layoff cannot be avoided. The only way to keep your best talent is to create a free-agent nation inside your department.

Your employees want to excel in three life areas: work, family, and self-realization, but it takes time devoted to all three to get the desired results. You surely are no different. Gen X and Gen Y employees see being a free agent as a way to reduce financial peaks and valleys. The corporate turmoil of the past twenty years played out in their living rooms as their parents and parents' friends talked about lost jobs or the stress and lack of balance in their lives. Gen X and Gen Y employees are willing to scale down their financial dreams to achieve balance. After September 11, Baby Boomers joined them in prioritizing family over—or at least on par with— work. Many Boomers will leave their full-time jobs well before age sixty-five to return to the workforce as part-timers, consultants, or project staff. Retired Veteran generation employees also seek time with family but are available for a variety of part-time and seasonal positions.

In "The Free Agent Declaration of Independence," author Daniel H. Pink says that the free-agent movement is appealing to your employees for the following reasons:[9]

- **Work is personal.** Employees believe that they will be happier and more productive if they are able to work and live as "whole people."

- **Nothing is permanent.** Job security is an illusion.

- **They have the power to say no.** Free agents can say no to difficult clients, underpaid work, or projects of no interest.

- **They have nothing to fear.** We have all spent too much time fearing layoffs or being blamed for things we did not do.

- **Work is fun.** Free agents think work is fun—serious fun!

- **They're on their own but they are not alone.** The community of free agents is growing rapidly. Independently, free agents are all together!

To engage your free-agent employees, find ways to expand their job responsibilities, move them laterally, and help them to move elsewhere within the organization. You can rev up employee productivity and retention by

- Taking a personal interest in your employees' careers

- Meeting with your employees to tell them, "This is why your position is important to the goals of the company"

- Helping employees to identify the skills they need to develop for moving to the next career step they desire[10]

If you spend time getting to know your employees as individuals, understanding their lives and aspirations, you have nothing to fear. You can create opportunities inside your department so that your employees feel like they do not have to leave to become free agents. They want to be energized by their work, and MOCs are energizers!

Manager, Develop Thyself!

The ability to work well with others tops the list of "must-haves" when management candidates are considered for a new position, according to research by RHI.[11] CFO's were asked, "Which single factor weighs most heavily in your decision to hire a management-level job candidate?" They responded as follows:

- Interpersonal skills (26 percent)

- Industry experience (21 percent)

- Proven accomplishments (19 percent)

- Years of experience (15 percent)

- Technical knowledge (12 percent)

Note that technical skills are not at the top of the list, but both interpersonal and technical skills can be learned and developed. While you cannot afford to be out of touch with technical developments, excellent interpersonal skills are essential for your primary job responsibilities. Your organization needs for you to be a persuasive communicator in leading and motivating your staff. Your organization cannot motivate employees without you. Your employees are (or are not) loyal to you, not the overall organization. SHRM research shows that senior management looks for performance (defined as *accomplishment of work*) and character (defined as *integrity*).[12] Use every opportunity to build relationships throughout your organization, grow your hard and soft skills, keep up with technology, and be conversant with the trends in your industry.

Tying It All Together

Employees make an average of one hundred unsupervised decisions a day,[13] so they need the skills and judgment to be able to have the majority of those decisions go well. Your role as a skill builder is critical to their—and your—success. Skilled employees are in demand, but skill builders are even more in demand because they know how to get work done well!

It is foolish to leave career development up to the employee. Walker Information and the Hudson Institute found that "care and concern," specifically in terms of treatment and their career, are critical influencers on employees' decision to stay with an employer.[14] If you leave skill and knowledge development completely to your employees, they will leave your department, and possibly the organization, to join a manager of choice who cares about them.

Every employee deserves to have a personal development plan, no matter how long they have been with the organization. Don't wait passively for annual training sessions for learning to occur. Development is an ever-building process. Skill building and knowledge growth must happen every day or our "learning muscles" get flabby and weak. Delegate, delegate, delegate! Expand learning and teaching options by asking your employees to take an active role in the skill-building process. Be creative when you reward and recognize employees for their progress and new capabilities.

Americans believe that in the future learning will be the most valued aspect of their life.[15] MOCs use skill building to attract top talent, improve productivity, maximize each employee's long-term potential, and plant great people throughout the organization and the industry when they move up or out. Nurture your relationships. Stay in touch. You *can* create future opportunities to work together. Skill builders are leaders who catch the eye of senior management and get promoted. By developing your employees' skills and engaging them in the learning *and* teaching process, you will also lower your stress level and enjoy your job.

Discussion Questions

1. What is on your agenda for your next departmental meeting? What are you going to add to it?

2. Besides English, what language should all your employees learn to make work flow more easily? What could you and they do together to increase your department's bilingual work vocabulary, understanding, and mutual appreciation?

3. Who should be invited to be on your department's learning task force? Should members of another department be included? How soon can you get the first meeting scheduled?

4. What is needed to coordinate your overall skill- and knowledge-building efforts with the formal training offered at your organization? Could a series of your departmental training sessions be compiled into a certificate?

Resources

To learn more about building employee skills and developing your staff to stimulate creativity and innovation, read:

Creativity in Product Innovation by Jacob Goldberg and David Mazursky. New York: Cambridge University Press, 1999.

First, Break All the Rules by Marcus Buckingham and Curt Coffman. New York: Simon & Schuster, 1999.

High Performers: How the Best Companies Find and Keep Them by Leon Martell. San Francisco: Jossey-Bass, 2002.

The Human Equation: Building Profits by Putting People First by Jeffrey Pfeffer. Boston: Harvard Business School Press, 1998.

The Learning Imperative, edited by Robert Howard. Boston: Harvard Business Review, 1993.

1001 Ways to Energize Employees by Bob Nelson. New York: Workman Publishing Company, 1994.

Up Is Not the Only Way by Beverly Kaye. Palo Alto, CA: Davies-Black Publishing, 1997.

Brand Builder

"What are you famous for?"

—**Dale Dauten,** author, columnist, and founder of the Innovation Lab[1]

An organization's product/service brand combined with its employment brand may attract top talent, but it is the manager's own personal brand that clinches the hire and enables engagement, development, and retention. Managers take action and make decisions every day that determine whether they are branded as ordinary or extraordinary, a manager or a manager of choice (MOC). What's it going to be for you? Ordinary brands are magnets for ordinary hires, making innovation much less likely. When the organization, department, or manager has an ordinary or negative brand, what would attract top talent? Top talent wants to work with top talent, including the best managers—and top talent gets to choose where it works.

Lower birth rates starting in the 1960s have so limited the number of talented people available that even in tough economic times, 90 percent of surveyed executives say that they have trouble attracting and hiring the best people for their organizations.[2] Top talent is attracted to organizations with a positive brand, and they accept offers from managers in departments with positive brands, or even—in the case of startups—the potential for a positive brand.

Ordinary managers distinguish themselves by what they fail to do. They stay within their budgets and get their reports in on time, but they fail to build relationships, trust, skills, and brands. If you are to be among the 10 percent who succeed in attracting and retaining top talent from inside and outside their organization, you must distinguish yourself by what you do to reinforce your organization's brand, and then shape your department's brand and set yourself apart by branding yourself as extraordinary: an MOC. Your role as manager is so critical to the overall organizational and employment branding process that you are either a brand builder or a brand killer.

For better or worse, each person you hire affects your organization's brand, your department's brand—and *your* brand. You cannot afford to hire an ordinary person to fill *any* job because *every* job in your organization ultimately affects the customer's experience. The brand extends beyond the actual product or service purchased. Each customer contact with your website, call center, accounting department, service team, and sales office either reinforces your organization's brand or becomes part of the process to change perceptions (positively or negatively) about your organization.

For each position, there is top talent—and it takes top talent in every position to ensure brand integrity. For example, baggers at a grocery store can destroy a shopper's experience or further enhance it, depending on whether they pack the bread and eggs on top of the cans or beneath them. Hotel housekeepers set the stage for a return visit by providing the guest with a sparkling clean room and a crisply made bed. Your organization's receptionist can either deaden or deepen a customer's or vendor's relationship depending on whether he or she cheerfully greets each call and visitor and confidently tracks down employees as requested. A prospect can be turned into a customer depending on the courtesy, speed, and content of e-mailed responses to questions. Every employee—not just the "top dogs"—affects a customer's experience and the organization's brand.

In this chapter we look at how organizational brands work with employment brands; how your organization's brands affect quality, efficiency, innovation, and creativity; and how MOCs collaborate with their HR and Marketing partners to go beyond organizational and employment brands to attract top talent.

The Organizational Brand–Employment Brand Connection

It can be difficult to separate organizational brand from employment brand—the two are inevitably linked. Achievement in one may serve to catapult the other. Positive and negative reinforcement are ongoing. A glitch in one becomes a hurdle for the other.

An organizational brand is an important intangible asset, sometimes called "hidden capital."[3] The brand includes the quality of the products or services sold, patents, the caliber of the organization's management and employees, and the sum total of its customers' experiences with the organization (such as the order experience or service experience). According to research by the Council on Foundations and Walker Information, organizational philanthropy programs are also an important element of an organization's total brand.[4] Reputation is part of the brand because it includes what customers, prospects, employees, and potential employees have heard about the organization, either from the organization itself or from other stakeholders (customers, employees, vendors, or investors). For example, while a hotel may claim to offer a "heavenly" experience, claims do not make the brand real. It is the customer experience itself that validates the brand and sends the value of the organization up the charts. In the case of Westin Hotels, their Heavenly Bed® is so "heavenly" that the sales of the mattresses, bed covers, and even the bed frame itself have become a separate profit stream for the company.

An employment brand is the labor market's perception of your organization's employment value proposition or compelling employment offer (why employees work there). At one time, simply being a big employer or making a well-respected product was enough to attract and retain employees. Today, because there are so many career choices and job alternatives, the value proposition "must be an accurate representation of what your current employees think it's like to work there."[5] Yesterday is history. Internet resources such as www.wetfeet.com, other business media, as well as stories from current and past employees provide trusted validation of the "official" story. The real experience of working for your organization is its value proposition. Today, an employment brand includes an organization's employer of choice status, its culture, structure, career development processes, compensation and benefits, rewards and recognition, hands-on community involvement and philanthropy, and recruiting practices. An organization's employment brand translates to its overall treatment of its employees.

Employees will leave if promises (such as the availability of flexible work arrangements, career development, or the opportunity to work on exciting projects) go unfulfilled. An employment value proposition that claims to include those elements would be invalid. The incongruity itself would become part of the organization's reputation and brand, thus hindering hiring. Again, managers who ignore elements of the brand become brand killers.

A strong value proposition can enhance employee satisfaction, ideally resulting in increased attention to product or service quality and increased customer satisfaction. Together, a positive employment brand and positive organizational brand such as that established by the U.S. Marines (see "What's Working" on page 193)

What's Working for the U.S. Marines

In tight hiring times, having a great employer brand is critical for the U.S. Marine Corps as it tries to set itself apart from its direct talent competitors (the U.S. Army, Navy, Coast Guard, and Air Force). By expanding its employer brand, the Marines were able to increase awareness among target hires and fill hiring quotas in spite of having one-fifth the hiring budget of each of the other branches of the armed services.

The Marine Corps built an employment brand on the foundation of values important to its target market and intrinsic to its existence: "the epitome of military virtue, a group of smart, tough warriors that gains strength of mind, body and character through membership in an elite and proud Corps."[6]

By branding the military experience with the Marines as an opportunity to acquire personal growth with messages such as "You will be changed forever" in addition to "The Few, the Proud, the Marines," hiring quotas are met year after year and retention is superior relative to other armed services.

improve the reputation of both your organization as a place to work and as a provider of products and services. In turn, your cost of hiring and cost of sales go down and profits go up.

Why Does Brand Matter?

Positive brands affect quality, productivity, innovation, and creativity because they positively affect recruiting results. Ultimately, brands matter to the bottom line. With so many talent competitors, so few Gen X and Gen Y candidates from which to choose, and Boomers and Veteran generation employees opting for part-time and alternative employment arrangements, cost-per-hire and fill times are increasing. The longer a position is open, the more negatively morale and productivity are affected and "domino turnover" increases.[7] Turnover begets more turnover and disrupts project deadlines, product introduction schedules, customer relationships, and profit projections.

A positive employment brand can minimize the degree of difficulty that your organization has relative to its talent competitors when it comes to attracting top talent. It increases candidate referrals by keeping the organization top of mind among school counselors, professors, and top networkers. A positive brand makes it easier to manage with WIT and rehire former employees for full-time, part-time, and project positions.

What Matters to Senior Management

Employment branding helps employees to embrace and internalize the organization's mission and values, and enhances the organization's reputation as an employer of choice (EOC).[8] If your organization can attract top talent—and out-hire its talent competitors consistently—it can take its place on the local equivalent of *Fortune*'s "Most Admired" companies list. More high-quality employees means higher profits.

What Matters to Investors

A company's market value now depends more on its people, brands, and technology.[9] In the case of publicly held companies, investors are stockholders; in the case of privately held organizations, "investors" may own a percentage of the equity in the company or may invest in the company by extending credit lines (vendors or banks). Some large corporate investors believe there is a link between people management and shareholder value. They demand information about retention rates, skill building, the use of competencies, and diversity. This information is often disclosed in private but is beginning to appear in annual reports as employers recognize its significance to their investors.

What Matters to Top Talent

As consumers of the work experience, top talent cares about brands. As the brand builder and manager, you matter to top talent. By what you say and do every day, you reinforce or undermine both the organizational brand and the employment brand. Your staff copies the way you model organizational values. People in the U.S. identify strongly with their job. Upon meeting for the first time we ask each other, "What do you do?" "Where do you work?" We cannot escape this link, so we feel that our employer's brand reflects on us. This is true for all generations of employees. Veterans want to work for a market leader, Boomers want to work for a leading-edge organization, Gen Xers want to work for a good corporate citizen that is family friendly, and Gen Yers want an employer that is family friendly and environmentally friendly. We all care what our peers think about our employer and our job.

If the organizational brand includes developing quality products to meet customer needs, but you, as manager, recommend cutting corners in order to deliver quantity, you are guilty of violating the organization's brand. Instead, brainstorm with employees for ways to increase production to meet a special customer need. If your organization offers flexible schedules, career development, an open-door policy, and other specific elements of the work experience, but you, as manager, do not encourage your employees to use these benefits, you are guilty of violating the employment brand. Instead, manage with WIT and ask employees how to get the work done while enabling access to work–life balance benefits. Misrepresentation of the organization's brand or the employment value proposition will lead to considerable employee dissatisfaction. Dissatisfied employees can become saboteurs but are most likely to do the minimum to get by ("quit on the job") or quit the organization altogether. No creativity or innovation can be expected from misled or dissatisfied employees, and their recounting of their negative work experiences outside the organization will damage your ability to hire replacements.

Attracting and keeping top talent will continue to be a challenge for managers in organizations of all sizes and types, so it is important to understand what attracts top talent—and to use those factors in job ads, on your organization's website, and in conversations with employees and job candidates. Table 8 shows a synopsis of a research report by Right Management Consultants in which 3,606 "high-value talent" respondents from twenty-six organizations described the "organizational brand profile" they desire from an array of twelve choices in each category. As you look at this research summary, ask yourself, "Do my employees believe that our organization fits this brand profile?" and, "Do my employees experience their work in our department this way?"

The exact value proposition may vary depending on the specific employee population. What is important for IT employees may be different from what is important for marketing staff, sales staff, administrative support, and others. MOCs listen for different interpretations so that they can deliver on the value promise.

Collaborate to Develop Your Department and Personal Brand

Since research from PR giant Burson-Marsteller found that the CEO's reputation constitutes half of the company's reputation,[10] it stands to reason that your reputation affects your department's reputation. Your Marketing department determines what is communicated about the organization's brand. Your HR executives hold the enhancement of the employer brand and reputation as one of their key objectives.[11] You must team with your peers to give you insights into building your department's brand and your own brand as an MOC.

Table 8 Brand Profile Most Desired by High-Value Talent	
Organizational Values	**Organizational Culture**
Make honesty and integrity the corner-stone of our spirit. Emphasize excellence in all that we do, and demonstrate caring in all our relationships.	There's no morale boost that beats work-ing in a team where creativity and innova-tion are valued.
Organization Brand Strength	**Organization Leadership**
Be known as a good place for talented people to work. Be known for superior quality and service as an industry leader. My reputation is on the line, too.	Set a strong vision, manage effectively to realize that vision, and keep me well informed. Tell it often and tell it straight.
Work Environment	**Compensation/Benefits/Development**
Giving me autonomy to solve problems when and where I want is great. But don't let go of the lifeline—keep me in the loop on changes taking place.	Competitive compensation is a deal-breaker. But, fairness in linking pay to performance and support for work–family balance are the real deal-makers.

Note: For each category of brand attributes, respondents were asked to pick three attributes (out of an average of twelve per category) that would be most important to them in choosing to join and stay with an organization.

Source: "People Brand: The Employment Brand Imperative," a research study by Right Management Consultants, Inc., Philadelphia, 2001, 6. © 2001 Right Management Consultants. All rights reserved. Reprinted with permission.

Twenty Ways MOCs Build Their Brands

In business, quality, efficiency, and speed matter. In these times especially, creativity and innovation matter also—so build your department and personal brands by deciding not to be ordinary or expected. MOCs do this using some or all of the following:

1. **Job growth and career movement.** Seek internal and external publicity for any new hires as well as employees who move lat-erally or are promoted. Listen inside your organization for job and project opportunities for your staff. Work with Marketing to send a photo with the press release to the employee's hometown

newspaper, alumni publication, and professional organization newsletter.

2. **Work–life balance programs.** Encourage use of available work–life balance programs such as flex-time, daycare referrals, and volunteering on company time. Offer to pilot new work–life balance programs first in your department before they are rolled out organization-wide. If an employee wants to job-share, consult your HR partner for ways to make it work. Become a model for the new employment relationship inside the organization.

3. **Respect and dignity.** Speak to every employee, make eye contact, introduce your employees to others who come to your department, and mention a positive personal comment so that you build your employees' personal brand with others in the organization.

4. **Communication.** Hold five-minute spontaneous stand-up meetings to update employees on current news; this will go a long way in dispelling rumors. Be sure to repeat the information in e-mails to off-site employees and at all your on-site meetings to ensure uniform communication and that questions get answered.

5. **Kudos.** Encourage employees to use a once-a-week collected kudos list to thank each other as well as employees outside the department for service "above and beyond."

6. **Awards.** Seek formal organizational awards for your employees and industry awards for your department. Don't let a deadline go by without a nomination. Mark your calendar! Create and pass out informal departmental awards as well.

7. **Rumor control.** Use anonymous e-mail for rumors and comments. Be sure to make all questions, comments, and your responses available to all.

8. **Conferences.** Seek speaking opportunities for you and your employees as well as opportunities for your employees to participate at trade show booths, especially where it will aid in recruiting for your department. At least monthly, find a way to send every employee to a professional organization meeting and/or a state-level conference. Host the professional organization meetings or committee meetings at your company, if possible. Investigate scholarships and grants, which are often available through professional organizations; discounted registration fees are often available for conference volunteers.

9. **Department chat room.** Set up a department chat room for employees to discuss technical questions and share solutions.

10. **Professional organizations.** Encourage your employees to seek certifications and to take leadership roles in appropriate professional organizations. Be sure that you do it, too!

11. **Community involvement.** Create an online or print directory of community programs in which your employees are currently involved, including employees' names so that those not yet involved can ask them about time commitment and other requirements. Be sure to list your own activities. Seek and share new opportunities for your employees to become involved in the community. Offer your conference room as a meeting place for committees. Seek opportunities for your employees to guest-lecture at local colleges, high schools, and grade schools, or to host school tours of your department or organization. Consider adopting a school or a class in a school.

12. **Departmental advisory board.** Ask current and past employees as well as peers from professional organizations to meet quarterly with you to discuss changes you are considering and to make suggestions to improve processes and increase innovation.

13. **Papers and presentations.** Encourage your employees to seek opportunities to be published or to make presentations to their professional peers. You should do it, too! Potential future hires will take notice.

14. **Case study articles.** Look for pertinent articles in your in-house newsletter, professional organization journals, alumni newsletters, and local newspapers. Work with your Marketing department to find the right examples.

15. **Department newsletter.** Create a department newsletter and use it to stay in contact with previous employees whose files are labeled "would rehire." Send it to your Marketing department for inclusion in the organization newsletter or e-zine.

16. **Photos.** Share photos of new hires so that everyone knows them right away. Create a scrapbook of department events or fill a wall with portraits of employees with their favorite things (family, pets, sports equipment, musical instruments, costumes, etc.). Take lots of photos!

17. **Logo'd company items.** Use company-branded items such as shirts, umbrellas, and supplies as prizes.

18. **Fun!** Challenge other departments to bowling or softball games, chili cook-offs, talent shows—whatever your employees think is fun!

19. **Learning.** Keep a running list of "what we've learned" as a source of pride.

20. **Family connections.** Invite families, vendors, other departments, top job candidates, and other friends to a department open house and tour. If budgets are tight, consider a "pitch-in" event. Pick a theme and ask employees to wear appropriate shirts, hats, buttons, or other props. Talk about the importance of your employees' work. Attendees will spread the word!

Reinforce Your Brands

In the past, discussion of an organization's brand or employment brand ended with the interview. Today it is critical to deliver on your organization's employment value proposition consistently from day one because new hires continue to receive offers to interview as well as job offers to consider. Keep it up because year two through year six are vulnerable to employee turnover. Until employees have been with an organization six years, their intent to stay is below year one levels. At year seven, intent to stay rebounds to year one levels and continues to increase.[12]

Re-recruit your employees regularly—your competitors are doing it! Tell your employees how valuable they are using your natural advantages as employer: weekly or biweekly meetings, ongoing e-mails and voicemails, chance meetings in the hall, as well as the twenty ways just mentioned. Celebrate your employees as individuals. Reach out regularly to reinforce the brand to off-site employees and teleworkers. Ask employees what and who cinched the deal when they came on board and why they stay. If they choose to move on, ask them how you could have done a better job reinforcing the brand.

If your organization is involved in the community and your employees have a favorable impression of your organization's philanthropy, they are *five times* as likely to stay as those who do not have a favorable impression of the philanthropic efforts.[13] Moreover, 88 percent of those same employees are extremely or very likely to recommend your organization's products or services, and 73 percent will recommend your organization as a place to work.[14] Make sure that your employees know about your organization's efforts to make your community a better place for all—and be sure to encourage them to participate.

Using anonymous e-mail or another anonymous mechanism, ask your employees what three things they tell their friends, family, and potential employees about working in your department. If they cannot recommend the department as a place to work, ask them to tell you what should change and why. Then get to work! This is your chance to be extraordinary!

Tying It All Together

When times are tough, budgets are tight, and staffs are lean, MOCs become brand builders in a big way. Your organization's reputation as an EOC is a key motivator that engages your employees' minds and hearts. A strong employer brand, and the loyalty it engenders, will carry you and your employees through the tough times and will make the boom times sweeter.

"For good or for ill, the reputation of an organization is made through the words and deeds of its members. That is the nature of accountability," according to James O'Toole, professor at the Center for Effective Organizations.[15] MOCs make sure that their department maintains a good reputation and has a positive brand within the organization, the professional community, and the community at large. To do that, they showcase the accomplishments, promotions, awards, and career and community development efforts of their employees by submitting their names for recognition and raising their profiles inside the organization, profession, and community. MOCs are anything but ordinary when they reinforce the organizational and employment brands by using everyday opportunities to model the values and demonstrate responsibility. MOCs are famous for brand building.

Discussion Questions

1. What is your department's brand in your organization? What is your department famous for?

2. What are you famous for? Use anonymous e-mail or other anonymous means to find out. Do your employees believe that you are a brand builder?

3. What is your organization's employment brand? What are you doing and saying weekly to support the brand? On the other hand, are you doing anything to undermine it? What has that cost you in greater turnover, lower morale, and reduced productivity? Reread chapter 2, "Managing with Whatever It Takes (WIT)," to find ways to support your employment brand.

4. Review the "Twenty Ways MOCs Build Their Brands." How many are you using? Ask your staff to prioritize the remaining list. Pick three and get them implemented immediately. Add three more every three months. Make a schedule marking your commitment to branding your department. Ask your assistant or a trusted employee to keep you on track.

5. How many of your employees does your supervisor or manager know by name? In the course of daily business, find reasons to introduce your employees up the ladder. Be sure to include a positive comment about each employee's initiative, creativity, follow-through, and so on. Find opportunities to build each person's brand to their peers and colleagues throughout the organization every day.

Resources

To learn more about brand building, reputation, and recognition, read:

Loyalty Rules by Frederick Reichheld, Bain & Company. Boston: Harvard Business School Press, 2001.

Promoting Yourself: 52 Lessons for Getting to the Top and Staying There by Hal Lancaster. New York: Simon & Schuster, 2002.

Stakeholder Power by Steven F. Walker and Jeffrey W. Marr. Cambridge, MA: Perseus Publishing, 2001.

"Emotional Branding" by Mike Hofman. *Fast Company* (May 2002): 70.

Conclusion: Making MOC Status a Reality

"Dwell in possibility."

—**Emily Dickinson,** poet

The start of this century brought with it a true break from the past: the future belongs to those who manage people well. Beyond the fact that managing people well is the number-one reason that successful companies make money,[1] there is genuine satisfaction in managing better than our predecessors. Today, talent scouting, relationship building, trust building, skill building, and brand building are the core competencies for managers in all functions in any industry. No matter what additional technical knowledge you need in your position, these are the five differentiators between being an ordinary, frustrated, outdated, "manage the numbers" manager and becoming an extraordinary, respected, successful manager of choice (MOC).

Whether you are in manufacturing, high tech, healthcare, retail, financial services, education, not-for-profit, or another field, your relationship with your external customers is changing. Your customers are becoming more knowledgeable and selective by the day, and the Internet is providing the gateway to global comparison shopping. Competition in your own backyard is significant, but nearly every organization is also feeling the pressure of global hypercompetition.

As organizations and their external customers change, so the role of the manager must also change. In your role as "people manager"—no matter what your level in the organization—your goal must be to manage better than anyone has ever managed you. Whether you work for a courier service with local customers, a utility with statewide reach, a manufacturer with national clients, or a high-tech company with potentially boundaryless clientele, you face the same set of challenges. Three external pressures on your organization—rapidly changing demographics, the emergence of the employees as consumers of the work experience, and the interaction of the organization's employment brand with its product/service brand—are shaping everything about the business, including the role and expectations of managers.

Today "One Size Fits One"

A number of factors—including the steeply diminishing numbers of available full-time employees with the retirement of Baby Boomers and Veterans, increasing immigration, and higher levels of education and participation of minorities and women in the white-collar workforce—dictate that the workforce will be growing increasingly diverse. Your organization's portfolio of top talent is its single best tool to beat the competition. Success will require focusing on individual employees and managing them individually with whatever it takes (WIT) instead of "one size fits all" benefits and work arrangements. Financially successful organizations will be staffed with a wide range of "A" players, men and women of different ages, races, religions, ethnic backgrounds, sexual preferences, and physical abilities requiring different work configurations—because that is where the top talent is!

As the overall availability of full-time top talent shrinks, employees are being recognized as assets instead of liabilities. Investors are increasingly interested in information about an organization's people management strategies and retention figures. Retention of top talent is seen to reduce costs and errors, increase customer satisfaction and employee morale, and prevent work overload. Multiple studies show that the value of an organization depends less on equipment and other tangibles, and more on brand, technologies, and people.

Veteran generation and Baby Boomer employees have spent the majority of their careers in an economy that grew too slowly to support the bumper crop of their highly educated and skilled peers. The "power of size" actually worked against those two generations because employers had the luxury of hiring from such a large pool of eager qualified candidates. Two decades of organizational turmoil at the end of the last century combined with the terrorist attacks and challenges of corporate governance, however, have left *four* generations unwilling to commit 110 percent of their life to the work world, especially when restructurings occur in good times and bad and so many organizations want to do more with even fewer people.

An unwavering desire for work–life balance and smaller total numbers have given Gen X and Gen Y an advantage: the "power of scarcity." Their determination to excel equally in family, work, and personal areas of their life, refusal to habitually work late, and desire to be active in the community are causing employers to reevaluate job descriptions and work configurations in order to hire the best talent. The alternative is hiring mediocre but available candidates who will repel the "A" players and only attract more "C" players. Employers have become "sellers" offering their employment brand instead of "buyers" cherry-picking top talent, due to a shift in supply and demand of the number of qualified employees versus number of jobs available. This reversal of years of employees force-fitting their life around their work is a relief to most but can be a source of envy for some. As a manager of choice, you must ignore the voices saying, "No one ever did that for me." Surely we all agree that a balance between work and life is better.

While all four generations are now being recognized as assets, employees see themselves as consumers of the work experience who are able to shop their skills to a variety of employers for use in full-time, part-time, project, telework, or consulting positions. The workplace is becoming more egalitarian and less linear and hierarchical.

Size Is Not a Recruiting Strategy

No longer able to use sheer organizational size to command customer market share—or employee "mindshare" and "heartshare"—organizations are looking for a magnet to attract more customers and talented employees. Senior management teams are realizing that their brands—both for products and/or services and for their employment value proposition—determine whether customers buy and return, and whether top talent even gives them a look.

Employee treatment is the magnet that pulls top talent to a specific employer. It also determines the quality level of products and services. With longtime corporate giants crashing to the ground, maintaining high ethical standards, too, has emerged as a key value as well as a branding element. The manager's deliberate role in modeling and rewarding the implementation of organizational values will further enhance both the employment and organization brands. You are the embodiment of the organization's culture as far as your employees are concerned.

Demographic changes, the rise of the employee as a consumer of the work experience, and the importance of branding are joined with two internal forces that are shaping the role of the manager: (1) the pressure to develop new products and services through innovation, and (2) the importance of people management skills to ensure a continuous pipeline of the best people for specific tasks, whether they are currently with the organization or waiting nearby. Great people managers—MOCs—are emerging as the heroes of their organization because they are the ones who inspire their employees to listen to customers for their definition of value and go beyond existing product quality and process efficiency to create new products and services that set them apart from their global competition. MOCs understand that just as customers demand a voice in defining value in products and services, scarce top talent also demands a role in defining value in the work experience. Table 9 shows examples of the old and the new definitions.

The speed of business has accelerated, and the employee's hunger for learning and meaningful work experiences has grown. As more candidates choose to be entrepreneurs or free agents with a variety of clients (including past employers), managers will need to hire—and later rehire—the same individuals several times in different capacities (full-time, part-time, project-based, and so on). In an effort to keep more full-time employees on-site, smart managers will listen for openings and projects within and beyond their department so that prized employees can experience a "free-agent nation" within the organization. MOCs' internal relationships with peers in other departments will facilitate the movement of top talent throughout the organization.

Soar Above Ordinary Managers

MOCs themselves will be able to move throughout the organization once they have mastered the five MOC competencies described in earlier chapters:

- **Talent scouting.** MOCs will be recognized for their hiring successes. Teamed with their HR partners, MOCs will out-hire their peers who fill openings with merely experienced candidates instead of focusing on the competencies of star players. MOCs will attract top talent by offering the opportunity to work with

Table 9 The New Employee Value Definition	
How Managers Define Jobs	**How Managers and Employees Co-Define Jobs**
Job Content and Job Description	**Work Content and Configuration**
Limited job availability publicity (frequently sequential posting: in-house intranet listings, word of mouth only, external posting only, passive signage, etc.)	Expanded job availability publicity (multiple simultaneous internal and external media postings: in-house intranet listings, employee/alumni/vendor referral networks, professional and civic organization listings and networking, etc.)
Rigid annual salary/wage increases (including variety of wage ranges depending on tenure, skill sets, etc.)	More frequently negotiated salary/wage increases (mini-raises at project end; spot bonuses; increased use of rewards and recognition)
Specific benefits (health insurance, paid vacation days, paid time off or personal days, uniforms, free parking, childcare vouchers, etc.)	Adaptable benefits (greater range available overall; longer list of benefits including training and fun will be offered to more non-full-time employees)
Consistent work hours/availability of work (full-time, part-time, 40-hour, regular overtime, etc.)	Flexible work hours/availability of work (negotiated by more employees; may vary from full-time to part-time or other configurations over the course of a year or by project; more alternative work arrangements of all types)
Conventional work environment/culture (one site or multiple sites, limited telecommuting, working out of the car, regular meetings with manager, etc.)	Fluid work environment/culture (more teleworkers, employees at multiple sites, virtual teams, etc., with increased use of technology to maximize communication)
Bureaucratic processes to define job content additions or changes (static or expanded responsibilities, use of technology, ongoing process improvement or elimination, timing of changes, etc.)	Rapid job content additions or changes (fewer rigid job descriptions; responsibilities keyed to values, initiatives, and projects instead of specific duties)
Longer tenure per position (fast-track position, dead-end position, development position, etc.)	Shorter tenure per position (multiple approaches; promotability tied to performance, not tenure; more project-focused time spans versus rigid "steps up a ladder")

other top talent throughout the organization as well as flexibility and alternative work configurations, and by ensuring that all employees have access to work–life balance benefits without fear of stunting their career options.

- **Relationship building.** MOCs stand out because their relationships give them access to a network of the best talent inside and outside the organization. Relationship-building skills also enable them to forge the alliances necessary with Human Resources, Marketing, IT, and other departments to ensure smoother daily operations.

- **Trust building.** For MOCs, 360-degree trust greatly enhances their productivity, as well as the productivity of others. Using their trust-building skills, they will be able to better communicate and elicit the intellectual and emotional engagement of their employees and peers as well as their own managers. Trusted employees, peers, and managers will not hoard information that can make the difference between success and failure with projects, other employees, or customers.

- **Skill building.** No one can afford to function with even two-year-old knowledge. MOCs know that exposure to new people and new knowledge is fuel for innovative thinking. Since the workplace is so dynamic, skill building can no longer be one-way, from manager to employee. MOCs teach their employees how to teach and join them in learning the latest technology, customer service techniques, financial ramifications of processes, competitive advances, and more. Certifications and other learning badges are as important for MOCs as for their employees. MOCs tap pockets of knowledge inside and outside their departments. They move themselves and their employees forward every day by constantly using different media to reinforce new learning and by building-in the use of new knowledge into performance management expectations.

- **Brand building.** MOCs who master talent scouting, relationship building, trust building, and skill building will become strong brand builders for themselves in the organization. As the embodiment of the culture to their own employees, MOCs understand that they are charged with modeling the organization's values every day. What they do must match what they and the organization say are their values and "how we do things around here."

Accountability is important at every level of the organization. By recognizing and rewarding all employees who not only meet financial or production goals but who refer top talent, seek community and organizational relationships, act in a trustworthy and ethical manner, and actively learn and share knowledge, MOCs develop a positive department brand. This brand quickly becomes known in the community of potential hires through the words and actions of MOCs and employees. In turn, this feeds the pipeline with top talent eager to be part of an intellectually energizing team.

Just as your external customers are demanding "interactivity, speed, individuality and openness,"[2] so are your employees. As an MOC, your responsibility is to support the strategic plan and accomplish organizational goals by managing your employees' experiences, engaging their hearts and minds to do much more than the minimum. When you succeed, you will be taking an active role in reducing recruiting costs and improving internal efficiencies that create value for both your employees and your organization.

The new consumers of the work experience define values when they seek work–life balance and opt for time off rather than a bonus, or part-time telecommuting to enable family time or the pursuit of a degree. You need to listen consciously to your employees to better understand their individual motivators so that you can ignite their imaginations and reap their best efforts. Your combined use of high tech and "high touch" will enable you to rise above the ordinary to become a manager of choice.

Notes

Introduction

1. "Emerging Trends in HR" (presentation by Keith Greene, director of organizational programs, Society for Human Resource Management, at the 30th Annual Ohio Human Resource Conference, Columbus, OH, September 26, 2002).

2. Dale Dauten, *The Gifted Boss* (New York: William Morrow and Company), 10.

Chapter 1

1. Jack Welch with John A. Byrne, *Jack: Straight from the Gut* (New York: Warner Business Books, 2001).

2. "Fallen Idols: The World Is Falling Out of Love with Celebrity Chief Executives," *The Economist*, May 4, 2002, 11.

3. From "The Towers Perrin Talent Report 2001: New Realities in Today's Workforce," www.towersperrin.com, 2001, 2.

4. Margaret M. Clark, "Hamel Shows Way to Cultural Innovation," *HR News Conference Daily*, June 27, 2001, 1.

5. Richard W. Judy and Carol D'Amico, *Workforce 2020* (Indianapolis: Hudson Institute, 1997), 101.

6. Jeffrey Zaslow, "Janis Who? Yesterday's Icons Don't Turn On Many Teens," *Wall Street Journal*, May 1, 2002, B1.

7. Pam Withers, "Retention Strategies That Respond to Worker Values," *Workforce* (July 2001): 37.

8. Steve Bates, "Best Practices Shared During First SHRM Executive Institute Forum," *HR News* (July 2001): 7.

9. Nancy S. Ahlrichs, "You Can Make Money Managing People," *Indianapolis Business Journal*, February 12, 2001, 48.

10. Ed Michaels, Helen Handfield-Jones, and Beth Axelrod, *The War for Talent* (Boston: Harvard Business School Press, 2001), 137.

11. Todd Raphael, "A Turnover Turnaround," *Workforce* (March 2002): 16.

12. C. K. Prahalad and Venkatram Ramaswamy, "The Co-Creation Connection," *Strategy & Competition*, no. 27 (2nd quarter 2002): 50.

13. From "Towers Perrin Talent Report 2001," 17.

14. "Life Cycle: Success Can Breed Vulnerability," *Chicago Tribune*, May 26, 2002, sec. 5, p. 6.

15. From the report by Towers Perrin and the Economist Intelligence Unit, "Business, People and Rewards: Surviving and Thriving in the New Economy," in "Towers Perrin Talent Report 2001," 9.

16. Gary Hamel, "What CEOs Can Learn from America," *Fortune*, November 21, 2001, 140.

17. "U1" column, *Fast Company* (July 2002): 72.

18. From Anthony Pantaleone, "Developing Effective Leaders," in "HR e-Lert" (newsletter, Business & Legal Reports, Inc.), www.blr.com, May 2002. Mr. Pantaleone is vice president of Profiles International.

19. Nancy S. Ahlrichs, *Competing for Talent* (Palo Alto, CA: Davies-Black Publishing, 2000), 2.

20. From Yoji Cole, "How Do Corporations Build Trust?" *Recruitment and Retention*, www.DiversityInc.com, March 18, 2002.

21. See "Human Capital As a Leading Indicator of Shareholder Value," in "Human Capital Index Survey Report," Watson Wyatt Worldwide, 2001/2002.

22. Frederick F. Reichheld with Thomas Teal, Bain & Company, *The Loyalty Effect* (Boston: Harvard Business School Press, 1996), 13.

23. Steven F. Walker and Jeffrey W. Marr, *Stakeholder Power* (Cambridge, MA: Perseus Publishing, 2001), 149.

24. Ibid.

25. From "Towers Perrin Talent Report 2001," 16–18.

26. Ibid., 16.

Chapter 2

1. Mark V. Roehling, Marcie A. Cavanaugh, Lisa M. Moynihan, and Wendy R. Boswell, "The Nature of the New Employment Relationship: A Content Analysis of the Practitioner and Academic Literatures," *Human Resource Management* 4 (winter 2000): 310.

2. "Know the Demographics of Your Workforce," in "Employee Recruitment and Retention" (newsletter, sample issue, Ragan Communications, Inc., Chicago), 2000, 9.

3. Diane E. Lewis, "Payday Doesn't Include Home Work for Most," *Chicago Tribune*, April 21, 2002, sec. 5, p. 5.

4. Gregory Weaver, "Curing Absenteeism," *Indianapolis Star*, April 14, 2002, E1.

5. Pam Withers, "Retention Strategies That Respond to Worker Values," *Workforce* (July 2001): 37.

6. See Humphrey Taylor, "Retirees' New Vision of Life After Work Years," *Indianapolis Star*, May 26, 2002, D4.

7. Figures vary. See Haya El Nasser, "Retirees Staying Put," *USA Today*, May 14, 2002, 4A; also Keith Greene, director of organizational programs, Society for Human Resource Management, "Emerging Trends in HR" (presentation at the 30th Annual Ohio Human Resource Conference, Columbus, OH, September 26, 2002), referring to AARP statistics.

8. T. Shawn Taylor, "Labor Shortage Isn't Benefiting Older Workers," *Indianapolis Star*, June 12, 2002, C1.

9. Jeff Fee, "Fathers Are Also Faced with Time Balancing Issues," *Indianapolis Star*, June 16, 2002, F7.

10. Kortney Stringer, "Time Out," *Wall Street Journal*, March 27, 2002, R14.

11. According to Sid Tuchman, father of a Harvard MBA grad who attended.

12. From "Long-term Care Insurance Improves Retention," in "Success in Recruiting and Retaining" (newsletter), www.nibm.net, 2001, 6.

13. See Ann Grimes' "Digits" column, *Wall Street Journal*, March 28, 2002, B4.

14. See May Wong, "Stay-at-Home Workers Extol the Benefits," *Indianapolis Star*, June 17, 2002, C3.

15. From "The Changing Face of Employment," in "Workplace Visions" (newsletter, Society for Human Resource Management, Alexandria, VA), www.shrm.org, vol. 1, 2002, 8.

16. Ibid.

17. Maria M. Perotin, "For More of Us, Temp Work Is Becoming Permanent," *Chicago Tribune*, September 15, 2002, 5.

18. From "Tap into Retiree Ranks for Experienced Consultants," in "Success in Recruiting and Retaining" (newsletter), www.nibm.net, 2001, 4.

19. See "Work More, Play More," *Working Mother* (June/July 2002): 17.

20. "Smart Moves," *Working Mother* (June/July 2002): 17.

21. From covers of *Working Mother* (June/July 2002) and *Kiplinger's* (July 2002).

22. Joe Radigan, "Remote Possibilities," *eCFO* (December 2001): 5.

23. N. Frederic Crandall and Marc J. Wallace, Jr., *Work and Rewards in the Virtual Workplace* (New York: Amacom, 1998), 56.

24. Ibid., 54.

25. "Flexible Scheduling Increases Employees' Attendance—and Productivity," in "Employee Recruitment and Retention" (newsletter, sample issue, Ragan Communications, Inc., Chicago), 2000, 2.

26. Wong, "Stay-at-Home Workers," C3.

27. From "Employee Involvement Is the Key to a Successful Work/Life Program," in "HR Focus" (newsletter, Institute of Management and Administration, New York), www.ioma.com, February 2001, 6.

28. Carroll Lachnit, "Relocation Changes to Fit Changing Times" (courtesy *Workforce*), *Indianapolis Star*, May 26, 2002, F7.

29. Wong, "Stay-at-Home Workers," C3.

30. From "Employee Involvement Is the Key," 6.

31. Ibid.

32. Stephanie Armour, "Workers Keep Tabs on Careers While Serving Their Country," *USA Today*, July 12, 2002, 3B.

33. Fara Werner, "Inside Intel's Mentoring Movement," *Fast Company* (April 2002): 116.

34. From Yoji Cole, "How Do Corporations Build Trust?" in "Recruiting and Retention" (newsletter), www.DiversityInc.com, March 18, 2002, 2.

35. Ibid.

36. Steve Jones, "When the Perks Fade," *Wall Street Journal*, April 11, 2002, B12.

37. Nick Gillies, "Work: Avoiding Knots When Learning the Ropes," *Observer*, August 22, 1999.

38. From Karl Ahlrichs, "Selling Ideas to an Indifferent World" (presentation at the 54th Annual Society for Human Resource Management Conference, Philadelphia, June 2002).

39. From "The Towers Perrin Talent Report 2001: New Realities in Today's Workforce," www.towersperrin.com, 2001, 2.

Chapter 3

1. Terry Deal and Allan Kennedy, *Corporate Cultures* (Reading, MA: Addison-Wesley, 1982), 7.

2. Jac Fitz-enz, *The 8 Practices of Exceptional Companies* (New York: Amacom, 1997), 67.

3. "Special Consumer Survey Report: Job Satisfaction on the Decline" (research study conducted by the Conference Board), www.consumer researchcenter.com, 2002.

4. Fitz-enz, *8 Practices of Exceptional Companies*, 71.

5. See Margaret M. Clark, "Hamel Shows Way to Cultural Innovation," in "HR News Conference Daily," Society for Human Resource Management, June 27, 2001, 1.

6. A. Mehabrian, "Communication Without Words," *Psychology Today* (1968).

Chapter 4

1. C. K. Prahalad and Venkatram Ramaswamy, "The Co-Creation Connection," *Strategy & Competition*, no. 27 (2nd quarter 2002): 54.

2. Nancy S. Ahlrichs, *Competing for Talent: Key Recruitment and Retention Strategies for Becoming an Employer of Choice* (Palo Alto, CA: Davies-Black Publishing, 2001), 14.

3. From "Craft a 'People' Profit-and-Loss Statement," in "Success in Recruiting and Retaining" (newsletter, National Institute of Business Management, McLean, VA), www.nibm.net, 2001, 7.

Chapter 5

1. From "The Towers Perrin Talent Report 2001: New Realities in Today's Workforce," www.towersperrin.com, 2001, 2.

2. From "Special Consumer Survey Report: Job Satisfaction on the Decline" (survey conducted by the Conference Board), www.conferenceboard.org, July 2002.

3. From "Practice Makes Perfect," in "Success in Recruiting and Retaining" (newsletter, National Institute of Business Management, McLean, VA), www.nibm.net, 2001, 5.

4. See Margaret Steen, "Employers Delve More Deeply into Workers' Pasts," *Indianapolis Star,* May 8, 2002, B7.

5. From Kipp Cheng, "McDonalds Website Golden on Diversity," www.DiversityInc.com, May 24, 2002.

6. See "The Impact of Diversity Initiatives on the Bottom Line" survey results in "Diversity Means Good Business, Survey Says," *HR News* (July 2001): 12.

7. Sigvald J. Harryson, "Why Know-Who Trumps Know-How," *Strategy & Business,* no. 27 (2nd quarter 2002): 16.

8. From Barbara Frankel, "Top 10 Companies for Diversity Recruiting and Retention," www.DiversityInc.com, May 23, 2002.

9. "Companies with the Times Lure Job Seekers in New Ways," *HR News* (April 2002): 1.

10. Karen J. Bannan, "Send in the Clones," *eCFO* (fall 2001): 45.

11. Craig Gray, "Employees A-Plenty: The Emerging Workforce of People with Disabilities," in "Mosaics" (newsletter, Society for Human Resource Management) 8, 1, January 2002, 1.

12. Sue Shellenberger, "Seeking Part-time Work: 60 Something Former Exec Will File, Answer Phones," *Wall Street Journal,* August 6, 2002, B1.

13. Shawn L. Berman, Jonathan Down, and Charles W. Hill, "Tacit Knowledge As a Source of Competitive Advantage in the National Basketball Association," *Academy of Management Review* 45, 1 (2002): 13.

14. These are some of the people management practices that when implemented result in up to 47 percent in total return to shareholders, according to Watson Wyatt Worldwide. From the Watson Wyatt Human Capital Index® study "Talent Management," www.watsonwyatt.com, 2001, 1.

Chapter 6

1. Hank Karp, Connie Fuller, and Danilo Sirias, *Bridging the Boomer-Xer Gap* (Palo Alto, CA: Davies-Black Publishing, 2002), 113.

2. Pam Withers, "Retention Strategies That Respond to Worker Values," *Workforce* (July 2001): 37.

3. ONEX, Inc., slogan, 1997–2001, Indianapolis.

4. Quotes from interview with Ken Martlage, president, Phoenix Images, Inc., May 9, 2002.

5. Jac Fitz-enz, *The 8 Practices of Exceptional Companies* (New York: Amacom, 1997), 14.

6. Michael N. O'Malley, *Creating Commitment* (New York: John Wiley and Sons, 2000), 235.

7. From H. Michael Boyd, "Building an Employment Brand and a Committed Workforce Requires Positive Symbols," Boyd Associates, www.brassring.com, 2002.

8. Withers, "Retention Strategies," 41.

9. Catherine Mercer Bing and Lionel Laroche, "Communication Technologies for Virtual Teams," *OD Practitioner* 34, 2 (2002): 12.

10. Interview with Bill Bagley, human resources and recruiting director, Deloitte & Touche, Cincinnati, OH, July 30, 2002.

11. Bruce Tulgan, *Fast Feedback* (Amherst, MA: HRD Press, 1999).

12. From Larry Bienati, "Rehabilitating the Problem Employee," www.brassring.com, July 5, 2002.

13. From a Pew Internet & American Life Project survey conducted by researchers at the University of Illinois at Chicago, in Martha Irvine, "Students Plugged In at Colleges," *Indianapolis Star,* September 16, 2002, A5.

14. Bruce Tulgan, *Winning the Talent Wars* (New York: W. W. Norton and Company, 2001), 32.

Chapter 7

1. Jac Fitz-enz, *The 8 Practices of Exceptional Companies* (New York: Amacom, 1997), 159.

2. David Enders, "FBI Has Launched a Probe of Kmart," *Indianapolis Star,* May 17, 2002, C1.

3. *The Economist,* June 8–14, 2002, cover.

4. Rob Kaiser, "Now a Few Words from the CEO of Frankness," *Chicago Tribune,* April 14, 2002, 1C.

5. "Employee R-E-S-P-E-C-T," *Business Finance* (September 2002): 15.

6. David Maister, *Practice What You Preach: What Managers Must Do to Create a High Achievement Culture* (New York: Free Press, 2001).

7. "Survey Says That Trust Is the Basis for Employee Retention," in "HR Focus" (newsletter, Institute of Management & Administration, New York), February 2001, 8.

8. Dennis S. Raina and Michelle L. Raina, *Trust and Betrayal in the Workplace* (San Francisco: Berrett-Koehler, 1999), 100.

9. Thad Green, *Motivation Management* (Palo Alto, CA: Davies-Black Publishing, 2000), 66.

10. Andrea Poe, "Family-Friendly University," *HR* (May 2002): 91.

11. James E. Copeland, CEO, Deloitte & Touche, in luncheon remarks at the City Club of Cleveland, August 16, 2002.

12. Pam Withers, "Retention Strategies That Respond to Worker Values," *Workforce* (July 2001): 41.

13. From "National Employee Relationship Report," Walker Information and the Hudson Institute, Indianapolis, www.walkerinfo.com, 2001.

Chapter 8

1. Graham Toft, "What the Heck's Going On Out There?" (presentation at the 8th Annual Indiana Human Resources Conference, Indianapolis, August 29, 2002).

2. From Tony Pantaleone, "Developing Effective Leaders," www.blr.com, May 2, 2002.

3. Theresa Minton-Eversole, "Demographics, Societal Trends Expected to Define HR's Future Agenda," *HR News* (July 2002): 5.

4. Toft, "What the Heck's Going On."

5. Interview with Bill Bagley, human resources and recruiting director, Deloitte & Touche, Cincinnati, OH, July 30, 2002.

6. From "Case Studies," www.skillsoft.com, September 18, 2002.

7. "E-Learning Dubbed 'Next Wave' in Sea of Training Options," *HR News* (July 2001): 8.

8. See "Smart Companies Support Volunteerism," *Computerworld*, October 16, 2000, 60.

9. Daniel H. Pink, "The Free Agent Declaration of Independence," *Fast Company* (January 1998): 131.

10. Susan Todd, "U.S. Workers Rethink Priorities," *Times-Picayune*, June 30, 2002, E1.

11. From a poll of 1,400 CFOs conducted by RHI in "Soft Skills Wanted," in "HR Fact Finder" (newsletter), December 2001, 8.

12. From a poll of 1,900 SHRM members in Margaret M. Clark, "Survey: Around the World, Business Values Same Top Leadership Skills," *HR News* (July 2002): 6.

13. "How to Prevent Misunderstandings," in "Working Smart" (newsletter, National Institute of Business Management), www.nibm.net, May 2002, 7.

14. From "National Employee Relationship Report," co-sponsored by Walker Information and the Hudson Institute, Indianapolis, www.walkerinfo.com, 1999 and 2001.

15. Sue Shellenberger, "Trends Point to Future of More Focused Work, Parenting and Learning," *Wall Street Journal,* January 9, 2002, B1.

Chapter 9

1. Dale Dauten, "Experiment Moves Innovation to the Top of the List," *Chicago Tribune,* September 15, 2002, C5.

2. From a website press release, "Attracting and Keeping Employees Still Tough," referring to "Sustaining the Talent Quest: Getting and Keeping the Best People in Volatile Times" (study by the Conference Board), www. conferenceboard.org, September 13, 2002.

3. Steven F. Walker and Jeffrey W. Marr, *Stakeholder Power* (Cambridge, MA: Perseus Publishing, 2001), 35.

4. "Corporate Philanthropy National Benchmarks Study" (employee report by Walker Information, Indianapolis), www.walkerinfo.com, 2002, 3.

5. From Bernie Eisenberg, Cydney Kilduff, Susan Burleigh, and Kevin C. Wilson, "The Role of the Value Proposition and Employment Branding in Retaining Top Talent" (white paper, Society for Human Resource Management), www.shrm.org/whitepapers, August 2001.

6. From Veronica Spencer-Austin, "Demystifying Employer Branding: Defining It, Developing It and Measuring It" (white paper), www. shrm.org, n.d.

7. Ibid.

8. Steve Bates, "Executive Briefing," *HR* 46, 12 (December 2001): 12.

9. From "Value at Work: The Risks and Opportunities of Human Capital Measurement" (study by the Conference Board), www.conferenceboard. org, July 2002.

10. From Matthew Boyle, "The Right Stuff," www.fortune.com/mostadmired, March 4, 2002.

11. From "Sustaining the Talent Quest: Getting and Keeping the Best People in Volatile Times" (study by the Conference Board), www.conference board.org, September 13, 2002.

12. "People Brand" (research report by Right Management Consultants, Inc., Philadelphia), 2001.

13. From "Corporate Philanthropy National Benchmarks Study," 3.

14. Ibid., 7.

15. James O'Toole, "Spreading the Blame at Andersen," *New York Times*, March 26, 2002, A27.

Conclusion

1. "Human Capital As a Leading Indicator of Shareholder Value," in "Human Capital Index Survey Report," Watson Wyatt Worldwide, 2001/2002.

2. C. K. Prahalad and Venkatram Ramaswamy, "The Co-Creation Connection," *Strategy & Competition*, no. 27 (2nd quarter 2002): 52.

Bibliography

Ahlrichs, Nancy S. *Competing for Talent: Key Recruitment and Retention Strategies for Becoming an Employer of Choice.* Palo Alto, CA: Davies-Black Publishing, 2000.

Badarocco, Joseph L., Jr. *Leading Quietly: An Unorthodox Guide to Doing the Right Thing.* Boston: Harvard Business School Press, 2002.

Barton, Kathleen. *Connecting with Success: How to Build a Mentoring Network to Fast-Forward Your Career.* Palo Alto, CA: Davies-Black Publishing, 2001.

Bell, Chip R. *Managers As Mentors.* San Francisco: Berrett-Koehler, 2002.

Bing, Stanley. *Throwing the Elephant: Zen and the Art of Managing Up.* New York: HarperCollins, 2002.

Buckingham, Marcus, and Curt Coffman. *First, Break All the Rules.* New York: Simon & Schuster, 1999.

Crandall, N. Frederic, and Marc J. Wallace, Jr. *Work and Rewards in the Virtual Workplace.* New York: Amacom, 1998.

Cripe, Edward J., and Richard S. Mansfield. *The Value Added Employee.* Burlington, MA: Butterworth-Heinermann, 2002.

Dauten, Dale. *The Gifted Boss.* New York: Morrow, 1999.

Davidow, William H., and Michael S. Malone. *The Virtual Corporation.* New York: HarperCollins, 1992.

Deal, Terry, and Allan Kennedy. *Corporate Cultures*. Reading, MA: Addison-Wesley, 1982.

Felkins, Patricia K. *Community at Work: Creating and Celebrating Community in Organization Life*. Cresskill, NJ: Hampton Press Communication Series, 2002.

Fitz-enz, Jac. *The 8 Practices of Exceptional Companies*. New York: Amacom, 1997.

Fritts, Patricia J. *The New Managerial Mentor: Becoming a Learning Leader to Build Communities of Purpose*. Palo Alto, CA: Davies-Black Publishing, 2001.

Fyock, Catherine D., A.E.P. *America's Workforce Is Coming of Age*. New York: Lexington Books, 1990.

————. *Get the Best*. Crestwood, KY: Innovative Management Concepts, 1993.

Goldberg, Jacob, and David Mazursky. *Creativity in Product Innovation*. New York: Cambridge University Press, 1999.

Goleman, Daniel P. *Working with Emotional Intelligence*. New York: Bantam Doubleday Dell, 2000.

Green, Thad. *Motivation Management*. Palo Alto, CA: Davies-Black Publishing, 2000.

Hacker, Carol A. *Hiring Top Performers: 350 Great Interview Questions for People Who Need People*. Alpharetta, GA: Carol A. Hacker Associates, 2002.

Howard, Robert, ed. *The Learning Imperative*. Boston: Harvard Business Review, 1993.

Ismail, Luby, and Alexander Kronemer. *Finding Diversity*. Alexandria, VA: Society for Human Resource Management, 2002.

Judy, Richard W., and Carol D'Amico. *Workforce 2020*. Indianapolis: Hudson Institute, 1997.

Karp, Hank, Connie Fuller, and Danilo Sirias. *Bridging the Boomer-Xer Gap*. Palo Alto, CA: Davies-Black Publishing, 2002.

Kaye, Beverly. *Up Is Not the Only Way*. Palo Alto, CA: Davies-Black Publishing, 1997.

Lancaster, Hal. *Promoting Yourself: 52 Lessons for Getting to the Top and Staying There*. New York: Simon & Schuster, 2002.

Maister, David. *Practice What You Preach: What Managers Must Do to Create a High Achievement Culture*. New York: Free Press, 2001.

Marofsky, Myrna, and Ann Johnson. *Getting Started with Mentoring*. Minneapolis: Ambassador Press, 2001.

Marshall, Edward M. *Building Trust at the Speed of Change: The Power of the Relationship-Based Corporation*. New York: Amacom, 1999.

Martell, Leon. *High Performers: How the Best Companies Find and Keep Them*. San Francisco: Jossey-Bass, 2002.

McKenna, Patrick J., and David H. Maister. *First Among Equals: How to Manage a Group of Professionals.* New York: Free Press, 2002.

Michaels, Ed, Helen Handfield-Jones, and Beth Axelrod. *The War for Talent.* Boston: Harvard Business School Press, 2001.

Neal, James E., Jr. *Effective Phrases for Performance Appraisals.* Perrysburg, OH: Neal Publications, 2000.

Nelson, Bob. *1001 Ways to Energize Employees.* New York: Workman, 1994.

O'Malley, Michael N. *Creating Commitment.* New York: Wiley, 2000.

Pfeffer, Jeffrey. *The Human Equation: Building Profits by Putting People First.* Boston: Harvard Business School Press, 1998.

Raina, Dennis S., and Michelle L. Raina. *Trust and Betrayal in the Workplace.* San Francisco: Berrett-Koehler, 1999.

Reichheld, Frederick F., Bain & Company. *Loyalty Rules.* Boston: Harvard Business School Press, 2001.

Reichheld, Frederick F., with Thomas Teal, Bain & Company. *The Loyalty Effect.* Boston: Harvard Business School Press, 1996.

Rosner, Bob, Allan Halcrow, and Alan Levins. *The Boss's Survival Guide.* New York: McGraw-Hill, 2001.

Seiling, Jane Galloway. *The Membership Organization: Achieving Top Performance Through the New Workplace Community.* Palo Alto, CA: Davies-Black Publishing, 1997.

Shurtleff, Mary. *Building Trust: A Manager's Guide for Business Success.* Menlo Park, CA: Crisp Publications, 1998.

Stack, Jack, and Bo Burlingham. *A Stake in the Outcome.* New York: Doubleday, 2002.

Terry, Robert. *Seven Zones for Leadership.* Palo Alto, CA: Davies-Black Publishing, 2001.

Thomas, David A., and John J. Gabarro. *Breaking Through: The Making of Minority Executives in Corporate America.* Boston: Harvard Business School Press, 1999.

Tulgan, Bruce. *Fast Feedback.* Amherst, MA: HRD Press, 1999.

———. *Winning the Talent Wars.* New York: W. W. Norton, 2001.

Useem, Michael. *Leading Up: How to Lead Your Boss So You Both Win.* New York: Crown Publishers, 2001.

Walker, Steven F., and Jeffrey W. Marr. *Stakeholder Power.* Cambridge, MA: Perseus, 2001.

Index

absenteeism, 39
accountability, 212
advisory board, 199
alternative work arrangements: and absenteeism reduction, 39; benefits of, 38; compensation determinations, 45; mentoring and, 48–49; need for, 36; structuring of, 42; success using, 39–41; types of, 43
assets: employees as, 4, 7–10, 93–95, 207
awards: brand building and, 198; departmental, 78–80; individual, 78–80; manager of choice, 85; organizational, 76–78; organizational culture promoted through, 76–80

Baby Boomers, 6, 30, 34, 132, 183, 195
background checks, 114–15
bad conduct, 149–50
behavior: earnings required to change, 131–32; inappropriate, 149–50
benefits plans, 31
blended teams, 154–55
boss: selling up to, 57–60; types of, 59
brand: building of, 197–200, 202; collaboration to develop, 196–202; employment. *See* employment brand; employment outcomes and, 67; importance

of, 193–96; investor benefits, 194; organizational. *See* organizational brand; personal, 57, 160; positive, 190, 212; product, 20–21, 65; profile of, 197; reinforcing of, 201–2; senior management benefits, 194; service, 20–21, 65; stonewalling effects, 164; top talent attraction to, 190–91, 195–97, 208, 212

Cawood, Scott, 161
coaching: individual approaches to, xii–xiii; relationship building by, 147–48
communication: brand building and, 198; of culture, 71–75; with employees, 135; of goals, 147; nonverbal, 71, 166; technology for, 151–54; trust and, 170
community involvement: brand building through, 199; skill building through, 182
companies: employment brand, 4–5; external changes affecting, 4–5; innovation focus of, 15; products as defined by, 11–12; scandals in, 3–4; strategic changes in, 5
competencies: brand building. *See* brand; description of, 18–19, 209, 211–12;

competencies, *cont'd*
  relationship building. *See* relationship building; skill building. *See* skill building; talent scouting. *See* talent scouting; trust building. *See* trust building
competency-based interview questions, 119–20
conferences, 199
confidence, 167
continuous learning, 19, 174, 176, 181
Copeland, James E., 170
counseling pairs, 153
creativity, 176
cross-training, 178
culture, organizational: awards for spotlighting of, 76–80; change in, 70; clues regarding, 66; cohesive messages about, 70; communicating of, 71–75; differences in, 64–65; employee involvement in creating, 68; expression of, 64; indicators of, 66; innovation in, 68–69; interview presentation of, 115–16; manager of choice's description of, 66; manager's role in creating, 65–70; new hire's fit within, 66, 112–14, 164; overview of, 63–64; personality assessments, 112–14; profitability and, 68; promoting of, 72–75; reinforcing of, 73; subcultures, 70–71; teaching of, 64; values of, 72
customer(s): boss as, 57–58; loyalty of, 23; products as viewed by, 11, 13; visits by, 178–79

D'Amico, Carol, 6
de J. Ruiz, Hector, 15
Deal, Terry, 64
decision making, 185
demographics: changes in, 4, 6–7, 206–7; manager's role and, 208–9
disabled employees, 125–26
discussion groups, 177
diversity: employee, 14, 121–23; job candidate, 121; methods for promoting, 121–23; skill building for, 175; top talent, 119–23
Drucker, Peter, 4

eldercare, xviii–xix, 35
e-learning, 179–81
e-mail: anonymous, 152–53, 201–2; prioritizing of, 153; reports delivered by, 144
employee(s): "A," 8, 10, 207; alternative work arrangement benefits for, 38; asset view of, 4, 7–10, 93–95, 207;

assimilation of, 95; bad conduct by, 149–50; behavioral triggers affecting, 10–11; caring for, 148; consumer approach of, 13; customer treatment of, xx, 19; customized work arrangements, 35–36; decision making by, 185; demands of, 14, 42, 192, 212; development of. *See* employee development; disabled, 125–26; diversity of, 14, 121–23; employer relationship with. *See* employee–employer relationship; encouragement for, 141–42, 201; expectations for, 149; and flexibility, 30–31; focus of, 183; free-agent status of, 183–84; full-time, 34; Gen X. *See* Generation X employees; Gen Y. *See* Generation Y employees; highly productive, 8; inclusion management for, 141–47; individual development of, 147; job definition by, 210; and job satisfaction, 67, 108; learning by, 148; liability view of, 7; life stages of, 13; listening to, 143–47; management metrics for, 93–95; manager relationship with. *See* employee–manager relationship; meeting with, 75, 144; morale of, 145; motivating of, 6, 31, 132; needs of, 26; nurturing of, 8–9; open forums with, 154; open-ended questioning of, 144–45, 147; organizational culture effects, 64; overworking of, 33; performance evaluations, 148; performance management standards, 8; preference variations of, 31–32; recognition of, 74; recruiting of, 95; referrals by, 125; respect for, 198; response to manager, 89–90; retention of. *See* employee retention; retraining of, xx; rewarding of, 74; satisfaction of, 167, 192; self-growth of, 148; shifting focus of, 10, 13; sick leave by, 33; stereotyping of, 142–43; support for, 141–42, 201; surveying of, 75; temporary, 126; turnover of. *See* employee turnover; unappreciated, 9; valuating of, 9–10
employee development: lack of focus on, 182; manager's participation in, 185–86; methods of, xiii; metrics for, 94; plan for, 186
employee retention: description of, 93–94; factors that affect, 163–64; methods to increase, 184; trust and, 163, 171
employee turnover: causes of, 192; cost calculations, 97–98, 100–101; detrimental effects of, 26; productivity effects, 97–98, 193–94; profitability

effects, 22, 193–94; skill building and, 174; tracking of, 9

employee–employer relationship: changes in, 29–30, 30; detrimental factors, 30

employee–manager relationship: building of, 18–19; changes in, 11–12; traditional view of, 11

employer: alternative work arrangement benefits for, 38; demands of, 42; reputation of, xx; workforce desired by, 30–31

employer of choice: criteria for status as, 20; employee recruitment and, 98; how to become, 20–22; manager of choice and, 20; manager's role and influences, xix–xx; people management recognized by, 90; reputation as, 202; standards of, 98

employment brand: building of, 19; definition of, 192; description of, 13–14; elements of, 192; importance of, 4–5, 65; job outcomes and, 67; manager's role in, 14; organizational brand and, 191–93; reinforcing of, 201–2; stonewalling effects, 164; trust in, 160; validation of, 192; violating of, 195

entrepreneurs, 209

EOC. See employer of choice

ethical standards, 208

expectations, 149

family: as employee priority, 6; work balance with, 34–35

feedback: consumer, 96; employee, 75; 360-degree, 95–97

financial performance, 134–35

Fitz-enz, Jac, 64, 68, 134–35

flexibility, 30–31

flex-time: evaluation of, 46; request for, 44; review of, 42

Ford, Henry, 7–8

Frankel, Barbara, 121

free agent, 183

full-time employees, 34

Generation X employees: definition of, 30; free agent, 183

Generation Y employees: attractive benefits for, 127; definition of, 30; free agent, 183; motivation for, 131

goals: communicating of, 147; mentoring, 54–55

Green, Thad, 166–67

Hamel, Gary, 4, 15, 68

Hierarchy of Needs, 23–24

hiring: Human Resources partnering to improve results, 109–16; success in, xx. See also new hire; recruiting

hiring process: background checks, 114–15; interviewing, 111–12; job application methods and processes, 109–10; personality assessments, 112–14; skill verification, 112

hoteling, 48

Human Resources: hiring results improved by partnering with, 109–16

humor, 60

Humphrey, Kathy, 80–81

Immelt, Jeff, 35

immigrants, 7

inclusion management, 141–47

innovation: culture of, 68–69; managerial focus on, 5, 14–15; relationship building and, 133–34; trust and, 161

instant messaging, 152

interviewing: competency-based questions, 119–20; organizational culture introduced during, 115–16; questions asked, 111–12, 119; skills in, 111

investors, 194

job: application methods and processes, 109–10; behavioral competencies for, 118–19; brand attributes effect on, 67; manager's definition of, 12, 210; soft skills for, 118–19

job candidates: application methods and processes, 109–10; background checks, 114–15; behavioral triggers affecting, 10–11; diversity of, 121; hiring of, 109; internal, 123–24; media advertising for, 126; mentoring-related inquiries, 49; and personality assessment, 112–14; professional organizations for, 125; rejected, 125; skill verification, 112; staff interviewing of, 138. See also hiring; hiring process; new hire

job description, 109

job growth, 197–98

job satisfaction, 67, 108

job shadowing, 178

Judy, Richard W., 6

Kennedy, Allan, 64

kudos, 74, 198

labor: demand and supply view of, 10

leadership forum, 84

learning: continuous, 19, 174, 176, 181; cross-training for, 178; customer visits for, 178–79; discussion groups for,

learning, *cont'd*
177; e-learning, 179–81; encouragement of, 148; job shadowing for, 177;
methods of, 177–81; research areas
for, 178; school alliances for, 179;
task force for, 176
life–work balance, 34–35, 60, 168, 170,
198, 207, 212
listening: relationship building benefits of,
143–47

Maister, David, 163
management metrics: and employees as
assets view, 93–95; important types
of, 91–92; reasons for changes in,
97–98; tracking of, 92; traditional,
90. *See also* performance management
manager(s): collaboration among, 80; communication by, 135; creativity of, 66;
employee focus by, 8; employee
response to, 89–90; employment
brand and, 14; individual approaches,
131; innovation focus of, 5, 14–15;
jobs as defined by, 11–12, 210; modeling of values by, 72, 163–68, 208;
organizational culture created by,
65–70; people management focus of,
16–17; performance goals for, 90–91;
profitability affected by, 23; rewarding
of, 15; role of, 14, 206, 208–9; self-
development of, 21, 184–85; senior.
See senior management; skill building
by, 185–86; style changes in, 6–7;
traditional training of, 16; values
modeled by, 163–68
manager of choice: awards, 85; book club
and exchanges for, 84–85; brand
building by, 197–200, 202; characteristics of, 190; community of,
80–85; competencies of, 18–19, 209,
211–12; definition of, 17–18; description of, 205–6; employer of choice
and, 20; importance of, 25; leadership
forum for, 84; mentoring groups,
82–84; organizational culture
described by, 66; people management
and, 26; recognition programs, 85;
relationship building by, 211; retreat
for, 85; skill building by, 186, 211;
tasks of, 159; and teleworkers, 47–48;
trust building by, 211; values of,
17–18, 163–68
manager–employee relationship: building
of, 18–19; changes in, 11–12; traditional view of, 11
managing up, 56–57

Martlage, Ken, 133–34
Maslow's Hierarchy of Needs, 23–24
matching, 164
meetings: employee, 75, 144; importance
of, 81–82; mentoring, 55, 83
Mehabrian, A., 71
mentee: mentor matched with, 50; training
of, 54
mentor: benefits of, 99; employee-specific
considerations, 50; role of, 51; selection of, 50–51; training of, 54
mentoring: activities to improve, 55; benefits of, 49, 61, 99; goals for, 54–55;
job candidate inquiries regarding, 49;
manager of choice, 82–84; meetings,
55, 83; new-hire, 49–50; peer-to-peer,
51, 82–84; program inception,
52–53; reciprocal, 51; success stories,
51–52; task force for, 52–55
mini–training function, 175–76
MOC. See manager of choice
motivation: employee, 6, 31, 132; performance and, 167–68

needs assessment: ongoing skill building
and, 174–82; telework, 42
new hire: bonding with organization,
135–41; mentoring of, 49–50;
organization brand effects, 190;
and organizational culture fit, 66,
112–14, 164; orientation of, 139–41;
relationship building with, 135–41;
retention of, 137–39; staff involvement with, 139
newsletter, 73–74, 200
nonverbal communication, 71, 166

open-ended questions, 144–45, 147
organization: accountability in, 212;
awards for, 76–78; culture of. *See*
culture, organizational; diversity of,
121–23; employment brand, 4–5;
external changes affecting, 4–5, 206;
new hire bonding with, 135–41; reputation of, 202; scandals in, 3–4;
stereotyping in, 142–43; strategic
changes in, 5; symbols used in, 142;
trust in, 162–63; values of, 165
organizational brand: building of,197–200;
characteristics of, 191; description of,
20–21, 65; employment brand and,
191–93; misrepresentation of, 195;
new hire effects on, 190; philanthropy, 191, 201; reinforcing of,
201–2; reputation, 191; self-reflection
in, 195; top talent and, 189; website
reinforcement of, 190

organizational culture. *See* culture, organizational

orientation of new hire, 139–41

O'Toole, James, 202

overtime: alternative work arrangements and, 40; need for, xix, 32–33

peer-to-peer mentoring, 51, 82–84

people management: benefits of, 17; employer of choice recognition of, 90; importance of, 5, 89–90; improvements in, 17; lack of, 7, 15–16; manager of choice effects, 26; manager's focus on, 16–17; profitability and, 22–25

performance: beliefs affecting, 167; financial, 134–35; motivation and, 167–68; trust and, 166–67

performance management: description of, 8; metrics. *See* management metrics; multi-rater tools for, 96; organizational culture promoted through, 74–75; relationship building through, 91; 360-degree, 95–97; values added to, 17–18, 74–75

personal brand: collaboration to develop, 196–202; description of, 57, 160

personality assessments, 112–14

philanthropy, 191, 201

Pink, Daniel H., 183

product brand, 20–21, 65

product development, 15

productivity: alternative work arrangement benefits for, 39; employee turnover effects, 193–94; methods to increase, 184

profitability: employee turnover effects, 22, 193–94; organizational culture and, 68; people management and, 22–25; studies of, 24–25

raises, 31, 132

recruiting: management metrics for, 95; organizational goals aligned with, 127; organizational size effects, 208–9; telework benefits, 40; top talent. *See* top talent. *See also* hiring; job; job candidates

relationship(s): employee–employer. *See* employee–employer relationship; employee–manager. *See* employee–manager relationship; hierarchy of, 133–35; morale and, 145; negative, 132; two-way nature of, 133, 155; types of, 133

relationship building: coaching for, 147–48; description of, 131–32, 211;

efforts for, 155–56; example of, 136–37; importance of, 18–19, 132; listening for, 143–47; new hires, 135–41; performance management for, 91; rewards for, 133; technology for, 150–55

religious accommodations, xviii

reputation: description of, 196; employer, xx; employer of choice, 202; organization, 202; organizational brand, 191

resume discrepancies, 114–15

retention: employee. *See* employee retention; new hire, 137–39; top talent, 14, 108, 156, 196, 207

Roehling, Mark, 30

rumor control, 198

salary raises, 31, 132

school alliances, 179

selling up: personal brand for, 57; strategies for, 59; understanding of boss for, 57–60

senior management: brand benefits, 194; innovation focus of, 5, 14–15

service brand, 20–21, 65

sick leave, 33

skill building: business goals and, 176–77; through community involvement, 182; description of, 211; diversity, 175; employee recognition for, 181–82; employee turnover and, 174; importance of, 19; learning task force, 176; manager, 185–86; manager of choice's role in, 211; mini–training function, 175–76; ongoing, 174–82; overview of, 173–74; rewards for, 181–82

skill verification, 112

soft skills, 118–19

stereotypes, 142–43

stock options, 31

stonewalling, 164

subcultures, 70–71

talent: hiring of, xx; importance of, xii; top. *See* top talent

talent scouting: description of, 18, 209, 211; and identifying top talent, 116, 118–19

team: assessment of, 145; new talent added to, 127

technology: communication using, 151–54; facts regarding, 151; impersonal nature of, 150–51; instant messaging, 152; relationship building using, 150–55

telecommuters, 35

telemanager, 47
telework: characteristics of, 43; getting
started with, 41–42, 45–47; implementation considerations for, 43, 45,
47; manager of choice tips, 47–48;
needs assessment, 42; recruiting
benefits, 40; request for, 44
360-degree manager performance management, 95–97
360-degree trust, 162, 211
Toft, Graham, 176
top talent: attracting of, 108, 190; brand
and, 189–91, 195–97, 208, 212;
competitors for, 109–10, 127; corre-
sponding with, 109–10; diversity of,
119–23; employer of choice preferences of, 21; identifying of, 116,
118–19; nontraditional sources for,
123–27; organization brand and,
189–91, 195–97, 208, 212; overabundance of, 30; retention of, 14,
108, 156, 196, 207; scarcity of, 6,
190; shifting focus of, 10; star competencies for, 118–19; value of, 4
toxic subculture, 71
training: business goals aligned with,
176–77; cross-training, 178; need for,
175; opportunities for, 31; values
added to, 75
traveling, 39–40
trust: communication and, 170; destroying
of, 165; elements of, 165; employee
retention and, 163, 171; employment
brand, 160; expression methods, 161;
importance of, 159–62, 211; improvements in, 165–66; performance and,
166–67; rebuilding of, 166; recent
business scandals that have affected,
162; success and, 168–70; 360-
degree, 162, 211; in workplace,
161–63
trust building: challenges for, 168; description of, xii; importance of, 19, 211;
strategies for, 170

Tulgan, Bruce, 156
turnover, employee: causes of, 192; cost
calculations, 97–98, 100–101; detrimental effects of, 26; productivity
effects, 97–98, 193–94; profitability
effects, 22, 193–94; skill building and,
174; tracking of, 9

value proposition, 192
values: manager of choice, 17–18; modeling of, 72, 163–68, 208; organization, 72, 165
Veterans, 30, 34, 195
videoconferencing, 155
virtual teams, 154–55

website: organizational brand reinforced
through, 190; tips for creating,
123–24
"whatever it takes" (WIT) approach:
alternatives, 37–48; description of,
32, 206; full-time employee reduc-
tions, 34; management changes, 33;
summary of, 60
women in workforce, xviii
work: flexibility in, 37; life balanced with,
34–35, 60, 168, 170, 198, 207, 212;
technological influences on, 37
work arrangements: alternative. See
alternative work arrangements;
customized, 35–36; flexible, 31, 33
work ethics, traditional, 32
work schedule: alternative, xix; flexible, 36
workforce: changes in, xviii, 35–36, 90;
demographics of, 4, 6–7, 206–7;
diversity of, 120–23; immigrants in,
7; increases in, 6; women in, xviii
workplace: changes in, 32–33; hours
required, 32–33; trust in, 161–63
Wyatt, Watson, 24